03 3162

IRVIN L. YOUNG MEMORIAL LIBRARY
WHITEWATER, WISCONSIN

3 3488 00141 6096

P9-EIG-875

DATE DUE

APR 0 2 2004	
ILL 4-'05	
DEC 0 5 2005	
ILL 10-'08	
11-2010	
ILL 4-'13	

GAYLORD   PRINTED IN U.S.A.

The Irish Potato Famine

Irvin L. Young Memorial Library
Whitewater, Wisconsin

GREAT DISASTERS
REFORMS and RAMIFICATIONS

The Irish Potato Famine

Carole Gallagher

CHELSEA HOUSE PUBLISHERS
Philadelphia

Frontispiece: As with many natural disasters, several events unfortunately coincided to create the conditions required for the Irish potato famine. Here, women search for potatoes, practically their only food crop by the mid-1880s. Many public policies and societal pressures also added to the human catastrophe.

CHELSEA HOUSE PUBLISHERS

Editor in Chief Sally Cheney
Associate Editor in Chief Kim Shinners
Production Manager Pamela Loos
Art Director Sara Davis
Production Editor Diann Grasse

Staff for THE IRISH POTATO FAMINE

Senior Editor LeeAnne Gelletly
Assistant Editor Brian Baughan
Layout by 21st Century Publishing and Communications, Inc.

© 2002 by Chelsea House Publishers, a subsidiary of Haights Cross Communications. All rights reserved. Printed and bound in the United States of America.

First Printing

1 3 5 7 9 8 6 4 2

The Chelsea House World Wide Web address is
http://www.chelseahouse.com

Library of Congress Cataloging-in-Publication Data

Gallagher, Carole S.
The Irish potato famine / Carole Gallagher.
    p. cm. — (Great disasters, reforms and ramifications)
Includes bibliographical references and index.

ISBN 0-7910-5788-7 (alk. paper)

1. Ireland—History—Famine, 1845–1852—Juvenile literature.
[1. Ireland—History—Famine, 1845–1852.] I. Title. II. Series.

DA950.7.G33 2001
941.5081—dc21

                                                2001032465

941.5081
G162

Contents

Irvin L. Young Memorial Library
Whitewater, Wisconsin

GREAT DISASTERS
REFORMS and RAMIFICATIONS

Jill McCaffrey
National Chairman
Armed Forces Emergency Services
American Red Cross

Introduction

isasters have always been a source of fascination and awe. Tales of a great flood that nearly wipes out all life are among humanity's oldest recorded stories, dating at least from the second millennium B.C., and they appear in cultures from the Middle East to the Arctic Circle to the southernmost tip of South America and the islands of Polynesia. Typically gods are at the center of these ancient disaster tales—which is perhaps not too surprising, given the fact that the tales originated during a time when human beings were at the mercy of natural forces they did not understand.

To a great extent, we still are at the mercy of nature, as anyone who reads the newspapers or watches nightly news broadcasts can attest.

Hurricanes, earthquakes, tornados, wildfires, and floods continue to exact a heavy toll in suffering and death, despite our considerable knowledge of the workings of the physical world. If science has offered only limited protection from the consequences of natural disasters, it has in no way diminished our fascination with them. Perhaps that's because the scale and power of natural disasters force us as individuals to confront our relatively insignificant place in the physical world and remind us of the fragility and transience of our lives. Perhaps it's because we can imagine ourselves in the midst of dire circumstances and wonder how we would respond. Perhaps it's because disasters seem to bring out the best and worst instincts of humanity: altruism and selfishness, courage and cowardice, generosity and greed.

As one of the national chairmen of the American Red Cross, a humanitarian organization that provides relief for victims of disasters, I have had the privilege of seeing some of humanity's best instincts. I have witnessed communities pulling together in the face of trauma; I have seen thousands of people answer the call to help total strangers in their time of need.

Of course, helping victims after a tragedy is not the only way, or even the best way, to deal with disaster. In many cases planning and preparation can minimize damage and loss of life—or even avoid a disaster entirely. For, as history repeatedly shows, many disasters are caused not by nature but by human folly, shortsightedness, and unethical conduct. For example, when a land developer wanted to create a lake for his exclusive resort club in Pennsylvania's Allegheny Mountains in 1880, he ignored expert warnings and cut corners in reconstructing an earthen dam. On May 31, 1889, the dam gave way, unleashing 20 million tons of water on the towns below. The Johnstown Flood, the deadliest in American history, claimed more than 2,200 lives. Greed and negligence would figure prominently in the Triangle Shirtwaist Company fire in 1911. Deplorable conditions in the garment sweatshop, along with a failure to give any thought to the safety of workers, led to the tragic deaths of 146 persons. Technology outstripped wisdom only a year later, when the designers of the luxury liner *Titanic* smugly declared their state-of-the-art ship "unsinkable," seeing no need to provide lifeboat capacity for everyone onboard. On the night of April 14, 1912, more than 1,500 passengers and crew paid for this hubris with their lives after the ship collided with an iceberg and sank. But human catastrophes aren't always the unforeseen consequences of carelessness or folly. In the 1940s the leaders of Nazi Germany purposefully and systematically set out to exterminate all Jews, along with Gypsies, homosexuals, the mentally ill, and other so-called undesirables. More recently terrorists have targeted random members of society, blowing up airplanes and buildings in an effort to advance their political agendas.

The books in the GREAT DISASTERS: REFORMS AND RAMIFICATIONS series examine these and other famous disasters, natural and human made. They explain the causes of the disasters, describe in detail how events unfolded, and paint vivid portraits of the people caught up in dangerous circumstances. But these books are more than just accounts of what happened to whom and why. For they place the disasters in historical perspective, showing how people's attitudes and actions changed and detailing the steps society took in the wake of each calamity. And in the end, the most important lesson we can learn from any disaster—as well as the most fitting tribute to those who suffered and died—is how to avoid a repeat in the future.

In Autumn 1845, a potato blight and famine began, changing the country of Ireland forever. For those five years, it lost its economy, main source of nourishment, much of its population, and its self-sufficiency. The cultural strife that arose from Britain's treatment of the starving Irish continues through today's political discord.

Sounding the Alarm

It was early autumn of 1845 and the village of Mionlach in western Ireland lay drowsing in the warm afternoon sun. Children played about the cabins, dodging chickens that scratched in the dirt. A few women sat chatting and laughing in the shade of a tree. A cow grazed nearby.

A man emerged from one of the cabins, spade in hand. It was Thomas Ward on his way to gather food for the evening meal. Thomas thrust his spade into the soil covering of his storage pit, expecting the blade to strike the top layer of potatoes. To his surprise there was no resistance. The spade was swallowed up to the handle. He pulled it out and tried again. This time he brought up a shovelful of foul-smelling black and rotten potatoes. Alarmed, he tested another part of the pit, with the same result.

The children stood still when they heard Thomas shriek the first time. As he continued to howl, they ran in his direction, as did the women. Before long, the whole town had gathered around him. Thomas Ward's potatoes had turned to mud, and no one could explain why.

■   ■   ■   ■

Thousands of farmers would make a discovery much like Thomas Ward's during the fall of 1845. After the leaves of potato plants began turning black in the fields that autumn, there was immediate alarm among the Irish peasants, whose entire means of subsistence depended on the crop. The potato was their main source of nourishment, and their chance for survival until next harvest

THE BLIGHT

Scientists now know that the potato blight is caused by a fungus named *Phytophthora infestans*. This microscopic living organism remains dormant in hot, dry weather. When it is warm and muggy, as Ireland often is during the summer, the fungus grows and spreads with startling speed; one plant can release several million spores in a day.

When it first attaches itself to a plant, *Phytophthora infestans* is whitish and barely noticeable to the human eye. The fungus quickly produces spores that attack and devour the plant's juices and tissues. The decaying black vegetation that results nourishes the fungus and it sends more spores through the air to other plants. When rain pushes the spores into the soil, they attach themselves to new potatoes and infect them in the same way.

The fungus can also infect potatoes that are healthy when they are dug up. If it is raining, the moisture can wash spores from the leaves of infected plants onto the surface of the healthy potatoes, activating the fungus. Within a few weeks, the potatoes will become black, rotten pulp.

Cold weather kills *Phytophthora infestans*. However, if farmers plant even one slightly diseased potato as seed the following year and the weather is warm and moist, the blight will continue.

The potato blight was caused by a fungus, *Phytophthora infestans*, that proliferated in the warm and moist Irish summers. The plants and potatoes themselves turned to inedible black pulp. Cold weather killed the fungus, but it was easily transferred to the following year's harvest through seed potatoes.

time would be slim without any potatoes from this harvest. Reports of diseased potatoes came in from many parts of the country. Even early-maturing varieties of potatoes that had seemed fine when they were dug up sometimes rotted later on in storage.

The Irish had grown potatoes for more than 200 years. Some believe the South American plant was introduced around the year 1600 by the famous English explorer Sir Walter Raleigh. Others believe potatoes may have been introduced even earlier—washed up on the beaches of Ireland from the wreckage of the Spanish fleet when it was destroyed by a storm in 1588.

Irish farmers found the potato crop easy to grow, requiring very little labor or training.

By 1800 Ireland had become the first country in Europe with the potato as its major food source; it was the principal food of the Irish peasants. The Irish were strong and healthy because potatoes contain enough carbohydrate and protein to supply almost everything the human body needs for good health, if enough are eaten. Although potatoes lack vitamin A and fats, most Irish ate potatoes with buttermilk, a byproduct of butter, which provides these essential nutrients.

Still, people who ate only potatoes needed a lot of them. It took as many as 14 pounds of potatoes a day to satisfy the hunger of a grown man. Arthur Young, an English agricultural expert who visited Ireland in the late 1770s, recorded the yield of potatoes in County Mayo as up to 12 tons per acre. A family of six required about five tons a year; therefore, if they held an acre of land, they could comfortably feed themselves and a few of their farm animals—a pig, a cow, some chickens—on potatoes. The potato could produce more food per acre than any other crop Irish farmers had grown before.

Although Irish potato crops had been ruined before by disease or harsh weather, this was a strange new kind of blight. The disease had migrated from North America, where it had destroyed potato crops the two previous years. Potatoes in England, France, and Belgium had also been blighted. In none of these countries, however, were people as dependent on potatoes as they were in Ireland. This potato blight, or disease, carried the potential for disaster because many Irish would surely starve without their main source of food.

The English government, which ruled Ireland in the mid-19th century, promptly asked a group of scientists to find the cause of this new blight. Since scientific knowledge was limited, the members of this scientific commission failed to recognize the blight for what it was—a fungus infection. Instead, they called it "wet rot" and blamed it on rainy weather. To solve the problem, the commission issued complicated new instructions for storing potatoes. Unfortunately, these were useless.

Experts also suggested ways in which potatoes that were only partly rotted could be made edible. But by the end of the year half of the potato crop had been lost, and the poor people in Ireland were immediately in danger of starving. In the mid 1840s, many of them had been close to starvation even before the problems created by this new disease. During the next few years, starvation, famine fever, mass evictions, and emigration became commonplace struggles for the Irish. This period of suffering became known as the Irish Potato Famine or, as the Irish more accurately call this time in their history, *an Gorta Mor*—"the Great Hunger."

Saint Patrick was responsible for bringing Christianity to the Gaelic tribes of Ireland in 432 A.D. Religion would continue to play a large and violent part in the country's history, especially when clashing with the neighboring imperialist power, Protestant England.

A History of Warfare

2

Ruins of ancient walls and monuments in the countryside stand as reminders of Ireland's long human history. An island nation located in northwestern Europe and surrounded by the Atlantic Ocean, Ireland claims Great Britain as its closest neighbor. It is possible that the first people, who arrived about 8,000 B.C., crossed from Scotland by a land bridge that no longer exists. In about 350 B.C., a fierce, warlike people, called Gaels, arrived. It is their Gaelic language and traditions that we think of as Irish.

Perhaps the most important event in early Irish history occurred during the fifth century, when the Gaelic people were converted to Christianity by St. Patrick. Born in England, Patrick had been carried off at age 16 and taken to Ireland as a slave. Six years later, he escaped, but he did not forget the Gaels.

After becoming a Catholic priest, he returned to Ireland in 432 A.D. as a missionary. Legend has it that he drove the snakes from Ireland, a story long considered a myth since the island of Ireland had separated from the continent of Europe before the age of reptiles, so there never were any snakes in Ireland.

When warfare shook the continent of Europe as the Roman Empire fell to Germanic tribes in 476 A.D., Ireland found itself protected because of its isolation as an island. Although centers of learning throughout Europe were destroyed during this time, the monasteries in Ireland remained safe havens. In them, monks guarded copies of the biblical Gospels, collected rare books in great libraries, and preserved a knowledge of Greek and Latin.

Still, the heart of Irish society remained the family, or more precisely, the family unit, or "clan." Typically a clan included four generations, from great-grandfathers and mothers to great-grandchildren. It was the clan, rather than individuals, that owned property. Several clans made up a tribe, and every tribe was ruled by a king. The warlike Gaels often fought amongst themselves.

As members of an agricultural society, the Irish people lived off the land. They were attuned to nature and the changing seasons. Most Irish made their living by grazing cattle. The young people took the herds to mountain pastures in early summer and lived there for the warm months. In autumn, they returned to their settlements in the valleys.

Each of Ireland's four ancient provinces—Ulster in the north, Munster in the south, Leinster to the east, and Connacht to the west—was ruled by a king with authority over the lesser tribal kings, or Irish nobility, of his province. Above all, at least in theory, was the *Ard Ri,* or High King. The High King usually had no power at his disposal but he represented the highest title of the land.

Vikings periodically attacked the island nation in the eighth century A.D. until they were defeated under High King Brian Boru at the Battle of Clontarf in 1014. Many invaders stayed in Ireland and gradually married and merged into Gaelic society.

Every noble household had a bard, a servant who worked as musician, poet, scholar, and historian. Irish nobility also relied on a brehon, who functioned much like an attorney and administered the Gaelic code of law, also called Brehon. The nobility practiced fosterage, a custom by which a child was entrusted for some years, usually until the age of 17, to the care of another clan with which the family was friendly. This practice created very close ties between clans.

In the eighth century A.D., outsiders from Scandinavia (a region of northern Europe that includes modern-day Sweden, Denmark, Norway, and Finland) began to attack Ireland. Arriving in warships, called longboats, fierce

Viking warriors destroyed monasteries and carried off treasures. Eventually, these invaders established settlements in Ireland—at Dubh Linn (Dublin), a name that means Dark Pool, and other harbors.

In 1014, Gaelic tribes joined forces under a High King named Brian Boru and defeated the Vikings at the Battle of Clontarf in 1014. After this victory, the invasions stopped, but many of the invaders who had already settled in Ireland remained. In time, they intermarried with the Gaels and were absorbed into Irish culture.

More warfare would follow. The next invasion came at the invitation of an Irish king, Dermot MacMurrough of Leinster. After losing his throne, he appealed to King Henry II of England, just to the east of Ireland, for help in reclaiming his title. Henry agreed and in 1170 A.D. sent an Anglo-Norman army led by a chieftain named Strongbow. However, after defeating Dermot's enemies, King Henry II decided to claim Ireland as an English possession.

Since few English people were willing to settle in Ireland at first, King Henry allowed the Anglo-Norman invaders to continue fighting the Irish tribal kings for their cattle and lands. Because the Anglo-Normans were a unified force and were better equipped than the Irish, they usually won these battles. Taking over the lands of Gaelic tribes, the Normans built great estates similar to those in England.

During this time some of the most powerful Irish kings managed to remain independent. Over the years, intermarriages between Irish clans and the families of the invaders took place, and the descendants of the Anglo-Norman invaders began to adopt the Irish way of life. Back in England, legislators responded to the Gaelic influence by passing laws in 1366 making it a crime for English citizens to speak Gaelic, dress in the Irish fashion, or marry someone of Irish blood. These laws, called

Ancient Ireland's four provinces, Ulster, Munster, Leinster, and Connacht, each contained (in ascending order) families or clans, tribes, and kingdoms. The four kingdoms were ruled over by the High King, Brian Boru, pictured here.

the Statutes of Kilkenny, created a physical and cultural division in the country of Ireland. Those who strictly observed the statutes lived within the Pale, an enclosed area bounded by wooden palisade fences originally built to protect Anglo-Norman cattle from raiders. Those living outside the Pale had adopted Irish ways and customs, and were looked down on.

In the midst of the constant warfare between the English and Irish, as well as the battles taking place between Irish nobles against one another, the rural Irish farmer had a great deal of trouble growing food to feed himself and his family. So the introduction of a new food source—the potato—at this time was welcomed.

Despite the animosities, the English, Normans, and Irish still had one thing in common—the Roman Catholic religion. However, in the 16th century, that changed as well when England's king, Henry VIII, renounced the authority of the Catholic Church in England and Ireland. To end his marriage with Catherine of Aragon so that he could marry another woman, King Henry broke with the Catholic Church and established the Anglican state church, or Church of England, with himself as head. Afterward, he grew increasingly intolerant of the practice of Catholicism in English-ruled lands. When Henry's daughter, Queen Elizabeth I, came to power, she proved to be even stricter in forcing her subject to follow the dictates of the Anglican church. Roman Catholic rituals were forbidden, monasteries were closed, and priests went into hiding. The Irish were forced to pay taxes in support of the Church of Ireland, although many continued to worship privately as Roman Catholics.

But religious oppression was not the only reason for the Irish to scorn the British. English authorities earned more hatred as a result of a government program called "plantations," which took land from its Gaelic and Anglo-Norman owners and gave it to new English settlers, thereby "planting" them on Irish soil. When the Irish mounted a rebellion to protest against this new policy, many of them were massacred. The hatred between the English and Irish was mutual. One English historian of the time noted that the English considered the Irish of so little value that killing one was regarded about the same as killing a mad dog. The uprising turned into nine long years of war, and ended with a victory by the English at Kinsale in 1601.

After Kinsale, the estates of defeated Irish chieftains, especially in the northern province of Ulster, were seized and given to Protestants from England and Scotland, driving the Irish from their homes and from land that had belonged to them for centuries. Sometimes, when no English wanted to settle these lands, the former Irish owners were permitted to remain, but as tenant farmers. In 1641, angry Irish Catholics in Ulster retaliated against the English by attacking Protestant settlements, killing men, women, and children without mercy. Protestant troops brought from Scotland responded with equal brutality.

In 1649 a new English army came to Ireland. At its head was Oliver Cromwell, leader of the Puritans who had overthrown the monarchy in England. Determined to wipe out all opposition to his government in Ireland, Cromwell spent the next three years subduing the Irish amidst wars, massacres, and plagues. Ultimately, the Irish surrendered and anyone in Ireland who could not prove loyalty to Cromwell lost his land. Thousands of Irish families were banished to Connacht, in the rugged western lands of Ireland. Cromwell's government exiled Roman Catholic priests from the country, and authorities had the power to remove Catholic children from their parents, and send them to England to be brought up as Protestants.

After Cromwell's death in 1659, his government collapsed. The English monarchy returned to power with Charles II as heir to the throne. Ireland's Catholic majority rejoiced, hoping the king would treat them fairly. Twenty-six years later, in 1685, King Charles's son, who was himself a Roman Catholic, came to power as King James II. However, many English lords feared the king's pro-Catholic policies, and asked a Dutch Protestant,

The English king, Charles I, was executed on January 30, 1649, by opposition leader Oliver Cromwell who sought to forcefully change the political, social, and religious life of both England and Ireland. Cromwell and his supporters followed a course of bloody and ruthless persecution against Irish Catholics. Thousands of families were exiled to the rugged western lands and priests became outlaws.

Duke William of Orange, to come to England and assume the kingship instead. Lacking support from the English army, James left England when William and his troops landed.

The deposed king withdrew to Ireland, where the large Roman Catholic population continued to support him and his claim to the British throne. Although James tried to rally his forces, he was defeated in July 1690 at the Battle of the Boyne. Afterwards James fled to France, but the Irish continued fighting for another year until one Irish leader, Patrick Sarsfield, helped negotiate the Treaty of Limerick. The document officially ended the fighting and promised some rights to Catholics.

Unfortunately, England did not honor the Treaty of Limerick. Instead, the British enacted severe penal laws against Catholics. They were prevented from holding government office, practicing law, bearing arms, and serving as officers in the army. Catholics could not serve apprenticeships, attend school, or leave the country to study elsewhere. They could not buy land, and men who already owned land were forced to divide it in their wills among their sons, thus reducing the size of their estates.

Some wealthy Irish families chose to become Protestant, at least in appearance, to protect their property. However, most Catholics continued to practice their religion, keeping their priests in hiding, and attending religious services, or Mass, in secret. In the country, religious services were often held at "Mass rocks, " which were located on high ground, so that approaching enemies could be spotted from a distance. Wandering Catholic schoolmasters taught the children at outdoor "hedge schools," hidden from view under high bushes.

The men who now controlled most of Ireland did not speak Gaelic or understand Irish customs. They believed that the Irish were uncivilized, lazy, and stupid people. Forced to keep their beliefs and practices hidden from England's law enforcers, the Irish became increasingly hostile to England and its oppressive laws. The Irish people had no incentive to work hard under British rule, for they were denied almost any kind of advancement and opportunity to pursue a better life.

Most of the Irish continued make a living as farmers,

At the request of English Protestants, Dutch Protestant Duke William of Orange wrested the throne of England from Catholic King James. James challenged William at the Battle of the Boyne River in 1690 but was defeated. This victory is celebrated to this day by Protestant 'Orangemen' in North-ern Ireland.

since there was too little industry in Ireland to provide many jobs. The great estates were run by managers, called agents, who hired tenant farmers. They in turn divided their farms and rented out acreage to several subtenants. These men divided their parcels and rented to peasant farmers called *cottiers*. The price of land became higher as it passed through this chain of middle-men, and the cottiers actually paid the most per square inch for their small plots.

Landlords received income from the rents, and agents also received a share of the profits. Many of these estate owners lived in England, and earned their income from the rents sent to them each year. English law also placed restrictions on the landlords, requiring them to hold estates in trust for their descendants. That meant they could not sell any of the land. If someone inherited an estate that had a lien (money owed to another creditor) against it, the new owner was obligated to pay the lien, even if he had to borrow even more money in order to do so.

Some landlords took the rent income and spent it on luxurious living. Others worked hard to improve their estates and help their tenants live more comfortably. However, landowners who tried to improve or alter agricultural production often met with resistance from the tenants. The landlord's idea of better farming techniques was usually based on the English model, in which each family lived on its own plot of land. This directly opposed the close-knit communal traditions of the Irish farmers.

In the 1790s, Theobald Wolfe Tone emerged in Ulster as the leader of a movement called United Irishmen. He attracted the support of Presbyterians and Catholics, both of whom were denied basic freedoms under British rule. In 1796, Wolfe Tone convinced the French to support an Irish rebellion. A French fleet sailed for Ireland to help the rebels make a surprise attack on the garrison at Bantry Bay; however, storms prevented the French ships from landing. The plan came to light and the Irish rebels were hunted down and tortured.

While the United Irishmen were battling for freedom, another organization—the Orange Order—was forming in opposition. The group took its name from William of Orange, and commemorated his victory over the Irish at the Battle of the Boyne. The Orange Order attracted those who feared and wished to prevent any Catholic rebellion. Such fears were realized in 1798, when Catholics in Wexford massacred their Protestant adversaries. English troops were quickly assembled, and they defeated the United Irishmen at Vinegar Hill that same year.

In 1800 Britain responded to these uprisings by passing a law officially incorporating Ireland into the United Kingdom of Great Britain. Although promoted as a step towards improving the lot of the Irish, this Act of Union effectively prevented any further attempts by Ireland to throw off British rule and establish independence. The Act of Union abolished Ireland's governing body of parliament, and absorbed 100 pro-British Protestants from Ireland into the British Parliament.

Eventually a few Catholics were elected to Great Britain's Parliament, however. Among them was Daniel O'Connell, who became one of Ireland's first national leaders. A lawyer from County Kerry and the descendent of an ancient Gaelic family, O'Connell had been horrified by the bloodshed he witnessed while a student in France during the French Revolution (1789–99). As a result, O'Connell refused to practice or promote the use of violence in gaining rights for the Irish people. Instead, he won power by forming political alliances in Parliament. He was also a gifted public speaker who won the trust and support of the Irish people as no one before him ever had.

During his tenure in parliament, O'Connell fought for the removal of the penal laws that prevented the Catholic Irish majority from receiving basic freedoms. After succeeding in 1829, he then worked to have the Act of Union repealed. Many other members of Parliament who depended on English authority to protect their interests opposed O'Connell's actions, as did the Protestant landlords in Ireland. A charismatic leader who appealed to the popular imagination and spirit of the people, O'Connell spoke at a series of public meetings throughout Ireland, urging that the Act of Union be repealed. His speeches continued to strike a chord with the people and his popularity grew.

In 1843, O'Connell was scheduled to appear at a huge rally at Clontarf, a town just outside Dublin. Thousands of Irish were already on the roads leading to the well-advertised event when the British government announced that the meeting was banned. Some advisors urged O'Connell to hold the rally anyway. However, aware that British troops were setting up artillery all around the meeting grounds, and the great likelihood of violence if the meeting was held, O'Connell ordered the people to disperse. His power and importance declined from that point on.

By this point in Ireland's history, political troubles and hostilities had been brewing for centuries between the Irish and English. But soon, decisions made over the freedom, rights, and quality of life for the Irish people would affect the very lives of millions more men, women, and children of Ireland.

The Irish Question

Old social and farming customs of Irish peasants in 1880 were in direct opposition to newer and better farming procedures then followed in England. The English landowners wanted to improve the efficiency and profitability of their fields, and the peasants stood in the way.

3

During the 19th century, visitors to Ireland were shocked to see hundreds of thousands living in poverty. Because the British occupied the country, its dreadful state reflected badly on England. In an effort to deal with the situation, the British government held the Poor Enquiry of 1835, during which authorities confirmed the terrible circumstances in which many Irish lived. Two-fifths of the population occupied one-room dwellings, typically built of mud, turf, or loose stone, and topped by thatched roofs of straw tied together with string. Because the cabins had no chimneys or windows and the Irish burned open fires for cooking and winter heat, poverty-stricken families lived out their lives in dark, smoke-filled rooms.

The poor, or peasants, had little or no furniture in their homes. They often slept on straw spread on the dirt floor. They owned few clothes or tools;

one witness at the enquiry told of three women who shared one coat among them. If a family was lucky enough to have a cow, pig, or chickens, the animals lived in the cabin too, and there was a pile of manure just outside the door.

Cottiers were the poorest farmers, forced to rely on agreements with subtenants for survival. In return for labor at spring planting and harvest time, a cottier received a small wage and a piece of land on which to build a cabin and grow potatoes. Over the years, as the Irish population had increased, the sizes of these individual plots of land had become smaller. By the 1840s, some families tried to eke out a living on only a quarter of an acre of land.

Some farmers had a better arrangement. Through a system known as conacre, they paid an annual rent for a plot of farmland. This method was popular because the rent was not due until after the crop was harvested. Payment could be made in the form of food or a farm animal, rather than cash. Conacre peasants built their cabins on unwanted land. After the men planted potatoes in the spring, they often left their families and country behind, in search of work on farms in England. Before the husbands returned in the fall, their wives and children were sometimes forced to beg in order to survive.

However they lived, the peasants remained at the mercy of landowners and their agents, or tenant managers, who were often unscrupulous. Raising the rents each year was a common practice, called "rack-renting." Since there was not enough land to go around, a peasant did not dare refuse to pay; if he lost his plot he would likely not find another.

Realizing that something should be done to prevent the further economic deterioration of the Irish, government leaders held inquiries and appointed commissions to address what became termed "the Irish Question." However, they could agree on no solution to remedy Ireland's agricultural time bomb, likely to erupt if the potato crop ever failed. To modernize agriculture, the land would have to be cleared of cottiers and conacre tenants, but the peasants had no other way to survive than to raise and eat potatoes. If large commercial farms were created, they would not provide enough jobs for all of the people who needed them. The English did not want to build new factories to create jobs in the country because a new Irish industry could then compete with existing industry in England. Also, British leaders and landowners were against giving any land back to the Irish.

To eliminate the poverty in Ireland, some government officials proposed encouraging emigration from the country to North America. During the 1800s, ship transportation had become more affordable because English merchants were importing timber from Canada and looking to fill the empty holds of their ships bound for North America. These ships were outfitted with wooden bunks nailed to the sides of their holds, and shipping agents began advertising in Ireland that inexpensive passage to the Canada was available. Irish emigration had begun to increase gradually, but until 1845 it was mostly the gentry and well-to-do farmers who made the journey. Most Irish peasants would not have considered leaving Ireland even if they could afford the passage.

After the Poor Enquiry of 1835, there was greater pressure on the British government to do something about the plight of the poverty-stricken in Ireland. Legislators responded by passing the Poor Law Act of 1838. Unfortunately, this act did not address the cause of Irish poverty; instead, it directed that workhouses for the poor be built and maintained. These workhouses were intended to be a refuge of last resort where people could go if they were evicted from their homes and had no where to go.

Within seven years 130 workhouses had been

It was cheaper for landowners to pay for tickets for peasants to emigrate to Canada or America than to continue to support them in Ireland. Travel posters were used to advertise passage from Dublin to New York and later, returning to the homeland. Many who made the trip to North America found it difficult to earn a living in such a hostile environment.

constructed in Ireland. The size of each workhouse depended on the population of the area it was to serve, although they were identical in design. Each contained separate dormitories and exercise yards for men, women, boys, and girls. Families that entered a workhouse could meet with one another only during chapel services on Sunday. A high stone wall surrounded the buildings. Altogether the 130 workhouses built could house one percent of the Irish population—about 100,000 people.

To discourage applicants, life in the workhouse was designed to be unpleasant. The British government succeeded in this regard—workhouse life consisted of extreme misery, and only the most desperate among the Irish fled to them. Up until 1846, only one-quarter of these institutions were full, even though the Poor Enquiry of 1835 had reported that more than two million people in Ireland were destitute. Rather than be separated most Irish families chose to endure hardship together.

The poor learned to survive with very little. They used peat from the bogs and swamps as fuel for cook fires and for warmth. They married young, had large families, and continued to enjoy communal life steeped in the customs and legends of their ancient Gaelic heritage. During the warm months, people went to fairs and festivals and met for dancing at the crossroads. When winter came, story-tellers and musicians entertained by the fireside. Travelers to Ireland before 1845 told of the warm hospitality they had received while visiting there.

Despite the country's poverty, the ample potato crop provided for the hungry. Every cabin had a basket at the doorstep, where boiled potatoes were left to drain. People didn't use utensils; potatoes were peeled with a thumb-nail when they were eaten, usually dipped in salt and buttermilk. Families well-off enough to own a dairy cow would churned butter from the milk to sell and then drink the buttermilk that was its byproduct. Leftover potatoes were made into potato cakes or left in the embers of the fire to be offered to any hungry visitor.

Children took cold potatoes with them to school to feed themselves and their schoolmaster. Fishermen carried potatoes with them to sea. In Donegal, the men carried stocking bags knitted by their wives to hold mashed potatoes. Laborers at work for a farmer gen-erally received as many potatoes as they could roast and eat at one sitting as part of their pay.

The system by which the Irish grew potatoes suited their growing conditions well. Farmers would cover a three-to four-foot wide area with fertilizer, then slice the turf through on each side, and turn shovelfuls of dirt over toward the middle to create a ridge between two trenches. This process sandwiched fertilizer between two layers of soil. Then the farmer dug holes in the upper layer and placed the seed potatoes inside. Finally, earth from the side trenches was piled on top so that the finished potato bed stood about a foot higher than the trenches.

The English called these potato ridges "lazy beds," criticizing this method of cultivation because it differed from their own methods of farming. On the extremely moist terrain of Ireland, however, the practice proved very effective because the beds allowed for good drainage in the wet lowland areas, which were often soaked by Ireland's heavy rains. The built-up beds also enabled peasants to extend their growing area far up on the rocky hillsides.

During the 19th century, farmers cultivated several varieties of potato in Ireland. They had names like rocks, cups, lumpers, pink eyes, leathercoats, and skerry blues. It is not certain how many kinds there were; the same variety was often called by a different name depending on the region in which it was grown. For example, what were called "rocks" in some areas of Ireland were "Protestants" in others, because Protestants had brought this particular variety of potato to Ireland.

The poor usually grew lumpers, also called horse potatoes. Coarse, watery, and bland, these potatoes grew well even in poor soil and without much fertilizer. They were also very large, some weighing as much as a quarter of a pound. Farm laborers who were digging a better variety of potato would be sent to a field of lumpers when it was time for their meal.

Most farmers did not consider potatoes a good cash crop. It produced no surplus—extra amounts that were not to be consumed and thus could be exported for a cash profit. Too bulky to easily ship, potatoes remained a local commodity. However, they could not be stored for an entire year; they would not last until the next potato harvest. Irish peasants referred to the period during each summer when the previous year's potatoes had either

been used up or were no longer edible as "meal months." During meal months people relied on grain (called meal) for food, or went hungry until the next potato harvest.

In England and America, the potato was highly regarded as a valuable source of food. In the first Webster's dictionary, published in 1828, the entry on the potato read: "In the British dominions and in the United States, it has proved one of the greatest blessings bestowed on man by the Creator." In fact, the availability of potatoes had made possible a population explosion among the poorest people in Ireland. Over a 50-year period, from 1791 to 1841, the number of Irish nearly doubled, to 8 million. At the same time the poor had abandoned the practice of growing crops of oats, barley, rye, and other vegetables, instead relying on the potato. Some historians believe the lumper and another variety—the cup—accounted for most of Ireland's potato crop in 1845. A few people pointed out that it was dangerous for so many people to be dependent on just one crop, but any warnings went unheeded.

Soup kitchens in workhouses replaced public works as the main distribution point for famine relief aide. But the kitchens, too, had flaws: the soup kitchens were funded by government start-up loans that had to be paid back; and the workhouses were already full to capacity, with not enough money to feed their inmates. Therefore taxes were raised substantially, putting even greater impetus on landowners to pressure the poor cottiers for rent money; the vicious cycle continued.

Peel's Brimstone and Public Works

The Irish farmers fought against rent increases as they spiraled deeper and deeper into poverty, hunger, and despair. The peasants were at the mercy of political, prejudicial, and economic forces that they little understood. The farmers' only hope was to earn a little on the public works, sell their belongings, and go into debt to buy enough food to survive until the Fall of 1846 and the next potato harvest.

4

One morning in 1845, Major Denis Mahon, a retired English cavalry officer, received an official-looking letter. When he opened it, Major Mahon learned that upon the death of a relative he had inherited an estate in Ireland. Without delay, he booked passage on a ship to Ireland and then traveled overland to Strokestown, County Roscommmon, in the western province of Connacht to inspect his new property.

The estate's manor house had been built in the 18th century, and Major Mahon noticed right away that it had a couple of unusual features. There was a long tunnel that ran beneath the gardens from the stable at one end of the house to the kitchen at the opposite end. When he asked what the purpose of the tunnel was, he learned that it had been constructed for the use of the Irish servants so that the English lord of the manor, his family, and guests would not have to look at them. The great kitchen at Strokestown also had a balcony, designed so that the mistress could drop her instructions to the Irish cook below without having close contact. The manor house exemplified the great barrier that Major Mahon's countrymen had created between themselves and the native people of Ireland.

As he spoke with local authorities and examined the estate's accounts, the major began to realize that he had inherited some difficult problems along with the land and buildings. Because the previous owner, Lord Hartland, had been insane for many years before his death, Strokestown Park had been neglected. Back taxes of £30,000 ($150,000) were owed to the government.

Because no agent had been managing the estate, the land had been divided into many small rental plots, but rents had not been collected from the tenants. The smallholders, as these small farmers were called, had agreed secretly among themselves not to pay Mahon anything. They resented him as an English outsider, and some claimed he had no right to the property. When one tenant broke ranks by offering to pay, the others threatened that Molly Maguire, a secret Irish society, would burn him to death.

Major Mahon hired his cousin, John Ross Mahon, as business manager at Strokestown. After studying the situation, Ross Mahon recommended that many of the smallholders be evicted and their plots of land consolidated to increase the size of farms for the remaining tenants. Ross also advised that the farmers grow grain, which could be sold for cash, instead of potatoes. In this way, the tenants would be able to pay their rents and the estate could become profitable again.

Knowing that those evicted would have no way to survive, Major Mahon was reluctant to follow his cousin's recommendations. So he did not take immediate action. But Mahon's financial situation soon worsened. In the autumn of that year, the potato blight struck, and he and the other landlords found that they had new taxes to pay in order to help support the local relief effort.

Relief, or welfare, like everything else in Ireland, was controlled by the British government. Within a few months, it became clear that the blight had affected at least half of Ireland's crop. When the extent of the damage became obvious, the government directed officials to set up the Central Relief Commission in Dublin and local relief committees throughout Ireland. These organizations encouraged private charities and wealthy individuals to make donations. The relief organizations used the contributions to buy food and distribute it to those in need.

The British Prime Minister, Sir Robert Peel, did more. He knew from past experience that if there was a shortage of potatoes in Ireland, merchants there would raise the price of other foods. That would only increase the hardship of the poor. Without telling other government officials, Peel secretly arranged to buy an alternate food source—Indian corn, also called *maize,* from farmers in the United States. He had this corn shipped to Ireland and sold by the relief committees a little at a time, at the low price of a penny a pound. If the merchants had known how small the supply of relief corn was, they probably would have gone ahead and raised their prices, but the secret was successfully kept. Because no merchants were selling Indian corn in Ireland, Peel could sell it without being

Sir Robert Peel, the English Prime Minister in 1845, began a government program to purchase Indian corn from America and sell it inexpensively in Ireland. Compared to potatoes, the corn was difficult to cook and digest, but it was better than no food at all. Peel's charitable action greatly alarmed merchants because it kept them from raising their prices even higher.

accused of competing with them. Even so, merchants later raised complaints against him for cutting into their profits.

Most British authorities believed that the government should not interfere with private business and was not obligated to protect and advance less fortunate subjects. Charity was considered a private and voluntary gesture of the wealthy. Peel's humanitarian action, modest though it was, took some courage.

In 1845, it took months for Peel's Indian corn to be shipped from America to England, and from there to Ireland. The people in the western part of Ireland, Connacht, were in need the most because the majority of that population had been the most dependent on potatoes as their source of food. Located in the most remote part of the country, Connacht had neither major roads nor good ports where the corn could be delivered by ship. The Central Relief Commission struggled for months to overcome these obstacles. It did not help that those in charge were employees of the British government who had little firsthand knowledge of Ireland or familiarity with the Irish people.

To buy Indian corn or other food, the poor needed money. So the British government established a public works program that created jobs. This system of aid had been used successfully in Ireland in the past. In March 1846 local committees bid on community construction projects such as new roads, docks, and other improvements. When projects were approved, the government loaned half the cost and then financed the rest by placing additional taxes on the wealthy residents of the locality. Some projects were worthwhile, but others were pointless, consisting of tearing up good roads and repaving them or digging canals that went nowhere.

By law, only one member of a family could be employed on a public works project. However, the wage paid was not enough to feed the large families that occupied most Irish households. There were also abuses, such as committee members awarding the jobs to their friends instead of to those most in need of the work. Still, public works kept many people alive.

With the money earned from these jobs, the poor bought whatever food they could afford. When they purchased Indian corn, which was unfamiliar to them, they had to be shown how to prepare it. Indian corn was nothing like the soft juicy corn used for food today. It was hard, dried, and so sharp that it could cut a person's intestines. Ideally, Indian corn should have been ground into fine meal before it was cooked. But the British government could not make successful arrangements for grinding Indian corn, especially in parts of rural Ireland, where the diet had consisted of potatoes for centuries and no grain mills existed.

Indian corn could be made edible by being boiled for a very long time to soften it. However, people often ate corn that was undercooked and then suffered severe abdominal pain. As a result, the Irish became suspicious of this unfamiliar food and would not even taste it until someone they trusted, such as a priest, had demonstrated eating it. The poor did not think much of Peel's Brimstone, as they called the corn, because of its yellow color. Nevertheless, it did keep many families from starving to death.

Within months, Sir Robert Peel's government fell from power. The new government, led by Prime Minister Lord John Russell, strongly maintained that the government would place no restrictions on free trade or intervene in economic affairs. This economic philosophy, called *laissez faire* (a French term that means, "let them do what they think best"), would be an important factor in England's future response to events in Ireland.

Sir Charles Trevelyan was Assistant Secretary of the Treasury—the man in charge of England's money. He and Sir Robert Peel had disagreed on how to handle the problems in Ireland, but Peel himself decided what aid the government would offer the

Irish. Once Lord Russell became Prime Minister, Trevelyan held that authority and personally directed all matters with regard to Ireland. He had to approve all expenditures. From the start, Trevelyan believed it was his duty to make sure that whatever aid was given to the Irish would be paid by Ireland.

The peasants, however, knew little of such matters of state. They earned what they could on the public works, sold their livestock and furniture, pawned their clothes, and went into debt. These measures enabled them to buy enough food to survive until the fall of 1846, when the new potato crop could be harvested.

Peel's replacement, Prime Minister Lord John Russell speaks during debate of the Reform Bill in the House of Commons, part of England's Parliament. Russell believed that government had no place interfering in trade or economic affairs. The potato famine was a political matter to him, not a humanitarian nightmare.

In July 1846 Father Mathew, a Catholic priest, noticed that the potato crop thus far appeared healthy. Little did he know that the blight would reappear that year and almost the whole country's crop would be lost. Here, he visits a farming family during the Great Famine. Such priests were a vital part of Irish society.

A Deepening Disaster

O n July 27, 1846, an Irish priest traveled along the road from Cork to Dublin, passing potato fields in full bloom. Father Mathew was relieved to think that it would soon be harvest time and people would have enough to eat again. One week later, his business in Dublin complete, Father Mathew set out on the return trip home. But this time, to his shock and sorrow, the fields he passed held a vast waste of rotting vegetation. In many places along the way, people sat on their garden fences, wringing their hands and wailing bitterly. The potatoes were blighted again, and this time almost the entire crop in Ireland was lost.

Within a month, the British government began receiving appeals for food from Irish relief committees and the government's officers in Ireland. Although a small amount of Indian corn remained from the previous year's supply, Sir Charles Trevelyan refused to release it. He did not trust the judgment of his officials in Ireland that the need for food relief existed. Trevelyan thought Irish farmers were trying to outwit the English and obtain free or cheap food. So, he made a rule that the government would not help in any region unless landlords and other wealthy people in that district first formed a relief committee and contributed money to it. One flaw in this plan was that often the landowners did not live in the area and did not know or even care about what was happening to the people of their district.

Trevelyan did order that the public works program be restarted. However, because he believed Irish people were lazy, he decided that rather than giving an equal wage to each worker, laborers would be paid for by piecework— the measurable amount they accomplished. This policy proved hardest on those who were most undernourished and most in need. Eventually the piecework rule was dropped because there were so many laborers and too few officials to monitor the necessary work records.

During previous food shortages, public works programs had been carried out only in the spring or summer. This time, because of the people's desperate need for money to buy food, the work programs continued during the winter. Poorly dressed, starving peasants walked for miles to and from the work sites, where they labored all day outdoors regardless of the weather. The combination of intense physical labor and harsh weather conditions burned up precious calories quickly. Some of these workers used their wages to feed their children instead of themselves, since a typical salary was not enough to buy food for everyone in the family. Some workers collapsed on the job, sometimes dropping dead from heart failure. They would be replaced quickly—every work project

Sir Charles Edward Trevelyan, English Assistant Secretary of the Treasury, personally controlled all relief efforts in Ireland after Peel's departure. Trevelyan believed any food and aide consumed by the Irish should be paid for by the Irish, and there-fore required local land-owners to found relief committees. The owners either didn't know or care about the starving peasants and did nothing.

had its onlookers, those without jobs hoping to be hired if a place became vacant.

As the number of people enrolled in the public works programs increased, delays in the payment of wages became more of a problem. The money could be as much as two or three weeks late in arriving. People starved to death while waiting to collect what they had earned. Pay clerks were tasked with the unpleasant duty of telling the laborers that they would not be paid on time. There were instances of clerks resigning rather than risking being attacked by angry crowds.

An unfortunate event occurred in Europe that year that compounded the disaster caused by the potato blight. Across the European continent in 1846, a poor harvest caused food shortages and high prices. The governments of France and Belgium addressed the problem by buying supplies of grain to distribute to their starving people. Some in Ireland called on the British government to do the same, but Prime Minister Russell, Sir Charles Trevelyan, and other leaders continued to follow the policy of government noninterference. Trevelyan had even been warned by grain traders not to bring in Indian corn as Peel had done the year before. This meant that merchants in Ireland could raise their prices, and wages earned on the public works now bought less food.

Many people could not afford to buy enough food to stay healthy, so they starved gradually or contracted diseases caused by a lack of nutrition. Deprived of vitamin C, people got scurvy. Their teeth fell out, black sores erupted on their arms and legs, and some died of gangrene as their bodies decayed. Protein deficiency caused small children to age prematurely while hair began to grow all over their faces. Older people suffered from famine edema, a condition in which their arms and legs swelled to almost twice the normal size. The lack of iron caused anemia, a blood disorder that left its victims extremely fatigued. Reports of men idling on the public works were likely due to this condition, although the English attributed it to laziness.

As in past times of hunger, people ate nuts, berries, roots, and edible weeds. On the western seacoast they were also fortunate to live off of shellfish and seaweed for a time, but eventually these sources of nourishment were used up. Captain Wynne, a British officer working on relief in County Clare, described crowds of women and children scattered over the turnip fields "like a flock of famishing crows." He recalled with horror how half-naked mothers and children scrambled across the fields as snow and sleet pelted them, screaming with hunger as they devoured whatever they could find.

As hunger increased, lawlessness did too. Hungry men attacked food convoys and storage places. Cattle, sheep, and produce such as turnips and cabbages were stolen. Some farmers shot thieves on sight. The usual sentence for stealing cattle was exile to a penal colony in Australia. Before 1845, such incidents occurred about 600 times a year in Ireland; by 1847, the number had risen to 2,000.

An early and fierce winter struck Europe in 1846. In Ireland, the winter months were usually mild. Some years, there was no snow at all. But in 1846, snow fell and icy winds blew continuously, beginning in November. Ordinarily, during the winter months the peasants stayed in their cabins to keep warm by the fire. Now, despite the harsh weather, they had to earn money for food at jobs at the public works dressed only in ragged clothing. The death rate continued to rise.

Starving fishermen lost the strength to go to sea in the harsh winter conditions that prevailed. Their fishing boats, called curraghs, were made of light wood and covered with animal hides; they could not withstand the stormy conditions. Determined to bring fish back to the island, some fishermen took the great risk of entering the turbulent waters and drowned. Many others pawned their nets and boats to buy food.

Pleas for food continued to pour into the Treasury Office in London from all over Ireland. In the rural west, where people had been most dependent on potatoes, starving peasants migrated to the towns. They begged on the streets and slept in ditches and doorways. Finally, on December 28, government depots in the west of Ireland were permitted to sell food. However, Trevelyan directed

The ocean provided some 'famine food' for the Irish. Fishermen rowed out to sea in their small boats, curraghs, but quickly depleted nearby resources. The boats were too tiny and lightweight to withstand the heavy winter storms or travel far away from the coast.

that people be charged the market price for the provisions plus 5 percent. There would be no price break for the Irish, even for those who were starving.

Many other parts of the country were also in serious trouble. A few weeks earlier, Nicholas Cummins, the magistrate of Cork, had decided to visit Skibbereen, County Cork, in the southern province of Munster. Since no one had formed a local relief committee, the town had not received government aid. Mr. Cummins heard in advance that the suffering was great in Skibbereen, so he brought along five men loaded down with as much bread as they could carry.

When the group reached the village, Cummins was surprised not to see any people about. He went into the first cabin, where he saw six people lying on some straw in a corner under a ragged horse blanket. They looked like skeletons, and at first he thought they were dead. As he came closer, he heard a low moaning sound. All of them—a woman, a man, and four children—were sick and feverish. Within a short time, the inhabitants of the village learned of the presence of men who had brought bread for them. Cummins later described the eerie scene: "I was surrounded by at least 200 such phantoms, such frightful specters as no words can describe, either from famine or from fever. Their demoniac yells are still ringing in my ears, and their horrible images are fixed upon my brain." Within days of this visit, another eyewitness wrote that there was a plentiful supply of meat, bread, fish, all foodstuffs at the market in Skibbereen—for those who could afford to buy them.

Mr. Cummins reported his findings to the government, but he received no response and no emergency supplies were sent. Sir Randolph Routh, the chief British relief officer in Ireland, blamed the 12 landlords of the district for not establishing a relief committee. Trevelyan suggested that Routh write personally to the landlords, detailing the degree of suffering among their tenants and cottiers on their estates. The British government was determined not to accept responsibility for millions of starving Irish or take significant strides in alleviating their plight.

Like the inhabitants of Skibbereen, peasants throughout Ireland began to contract famine fever. During that frigid winter of 1846–47, they gathered at the public works sites, in soup kitchens, and in their cabins, where they huddled together for warmth. Starvation was blamed for the fever, because it spread during times of famine. Not even doctors knew then that lice were the actual cause of the fever. Weakened by hunger, the Irish peasants were living in very unsanitary conditions. Because they had sold or pawned everything but the clothes they were wearing, they could not wash and change their garments. Wherever they congregated, their lice-infested clothes transferred disease from one to another.

Famine fever was actually two diseases—typhus and relapsing fever. Both were highly contagious. Simply inhaling air in which lice excretions had turned to dust could infect a person. The Irish called typhus "black fever," because victims turned a dark color. The illness killed two of every three people who contracted it. Relapsing fever caused deadly high fever and vomiting, which could recur, if the patient survived, as many as three or four times.

Yet another deadly disease that attacked famine victims was dysentery, called "bloody flux." It was spread by polluted water and food that had not been cooked properly or that had been cooked by people who were infectious.

Before 1845, there were only 28 hospitals in all of Ireland and about 500 dispensaries. Some areas did not have either. In these regions, the infirmary of the local workhouse became the area's medical facility. But workhouse infirmaries had been designed to care for just a few people at a time. And as the fever epidemic swept across Ireland, workhouse staff proved inadequate to take care of the sick, and government funding didn't provide enough money to buy food for them. Workhouse authorities could not even keep the sick separated from healthy people.

In March 1847 the Central Board of Health sent doctors to inspect workhouses and hospitals in the

towns of Cork and Bantry, in the south of Ireland. They found that at the workhouse infirmary in Cork someone was dying every hour. The high mortality rate meant additional manpower and resources were needed to bury the dead, as well as care for the sick. In their report on the fever hospital at Bantry, the doctors noted that the living and dead were lying together, naked, on straw. The doctor in charge was himself ill, and the only attendant was an untrained Irish nurse. There were no medicines, food and drink, or fire for warmth.

The epidemic did not strike all at once across Ireland. Instead, it broke out at different times in separate communities. Cecil Woodham-Smith, who wrote a comprehensive

Starving peasants outside the gates of a workhouse. Conditions and requirements at such houses were deplorable. Families had to give up their land (and any chance of future livelihood) to gain entrance; relatives were separated by gender; and healthy people slept next to sick patients. It was the last resort for most people, and their stay usually ended in death.

history of the famine, reached the conclusion that the fever was spread by homeless beggars, roaming from one place to another and carrying infected lice. In support of this theory, the author cited small villages, far from any main roads and unlikely to have been visited by itinerant beggars, that escaped the fever entirely, even though the inhabitants starved.

In response to the terrible need, the British Parliament passed the Irish Fever Act that April. The law authorized relief committees to set up, at government expense, temporary fever hospitals and make arrangements to bury the dead. Eventually, as the number of stricken patients outstripped all available facilities, British army tents were provided as temporary housing.

Records kept at the time suggest that the fever epidemic reached its peak in the workhouses and hospitals during April 1847. Some 2,613 inmates of workhouses died in just one week. Moreover, out of 990 people living in one workhouse, 830 had contracted famine fever. Incredibly, because these statistics were collected during chaotic conditions, many historians consider them to be lower than the actual figures.

By September 1847, the epidemic began to subside in the country at large although famine fever continued to run its course in certain areas of Ireland for several more years. It is estimated that 10 times as many people died of disease as did from starvation. Because so many died anonymously, however, there will never be certainty about the numbers.

Many of the starving poor refused to go to the workhouses, not only because they were unpleasant places but also because so many inmates died in them. The Irish were correct in believing that people who were healthy when they entered a workhouse were likely to become infected there. When people fell ill at home, everyone but the members of the immediate family kept away, know-ing the fever was contagious. Neighbors would not enter the cabin. Even family members sometimes put food and drink on a long-handled shovel and passed it to their stricken kin, rather than risk close contact.

As illness struck communities, fear of infection kept people from reaching out to one another in their customary way. Many people died alone, even though neighbors were nearby. Irish folklore is largely silent on this subject, because survivors of the famine were left with feelings of guilt and horror that customary religious and social customs surrounding a person's death were not carried out.

The practices involving the death and burial of a member of the community were very important to the Irish. Many a poor man had money set aside so that his funeral could be as fine as possible, with food and drink for the mourners and a horse and cart to carry his coffin to the church graveyard. However, during the famine, as the number of dead multiplied day by day, it became impossible for mourners to perform customary burial rites and rituals. As the number of deaths rose, family members made do with reusable coffins—constructed with hinged bottoms. People were buried in mass graves in the churchyards, fields, ditches, and hillsides. Some-times their cabins were simply pulled down over their bodies. An Irish storyteller alluded to this when she said, "no matter where in Ventry churchyard, big as it is, you might dig a hole, you would find bones because they were buried there without coffins or sheets."

A French chef from an elite London club, Alexis Soyer, set up a model kitchen in Dublin with an inexpensive recipe for soup. The kitchen fed over a million people during the famine; recipients had to meet strict poverty requirements. Wealthy benefactors considered the kitchens to be both charity and amusing entertainment.

Soup Kitchens and Tumbled Cabins

6

During the winter of 1846 and spring of 1847, protesters and rioters filled the streets of Irish port cities as ships there were loaded full of Irish food—oats, wheat, pigs, cattle, butter, and eggs—to be sold in England. The government responded by ordering cavalry and infantry soldiers to guard the ships until they sailed.

Even some British relief officials did not understand why Irish farmers and their families did not eat the grain they had grown. The fact was that these foodstuffs had been raised to pay the rent owed to English landlords. Even if his own children were starving, an Irish farmer continued to sell his crops so he and his family would not be evicted from their land, for then they would have no way to survive.

By January 1847, Sir Charles Trevelyan had finally been convinced that a dire emergency existed in Ireland. Aware that the supply of Indian corn left in the government stores was too small to meet the needs of the hungry and was priced too high, he closed down that relief program and replaced it with a program to provide soup kitchens. As the kitchens came into operation, it was decided, the public works would be gradually discontinued. British authorities reasoned that since people would be fed free soup they would no longer need wages.

The program established committees throughout Ireland that would set up and run the kitchens. The government provided start-up funds, but only as a loan that would be repaid by collecting taxes from the Irish. Unfortunately, the soup kitchen plan had serious flaws. Workhouses had been designated as the distribution centers for a free daily meal to people in their districts. However, the workhouses were already overcrowded and short of funds to feed even their inmates. Furthermore, workhouses were funded from local taxes, which had to be raised significantly to pay back the government's soup kitchen loan. In many districts it was already difficult for tax collectors to obtain money; they often found it necessary to bring along British police or soldiers to force even partial payments.

Some members of England's Parliament protested British policy in Ireland, arguing that the Irish had been abandoned and left to suffer and die after being denied the most basic rights by the British for centuries. Those who controlled the government, however, chose to regard the blight on the potatoes as the will of God. Trevelyan wrote that he hoped the Irish people understood that they were "suffering from an affliction of God's providence." If this was God's will, many British leaders reasoned, then England was blameless and ought not to interfere regardless of the outcome. This way of thinking coincided with the government's policy of laissez faire—to let events run their course without interference. And British policy reflected the government's long-term interests for land reform in Ireland, which would be possible if the Irish population was reduced, thus clearing the land for agricultural reform. Some British leaders believed that the Irish Question would be resolved by allowing nature to starve the Irish out of the landscape.

Because the public works program cost England a great deal of money, the government was anxious to close it down. Administration of the public works required a large staff to oversee the rapidly increasing Irish labor force. In October 1846, 114,000 men had been employed. Three months later, as more and more peasants were forced off their land, the labor force more than quadrupled to 570,000. By March 1847, the total reached 734,000 men, women, and children, and the daily cost of the public works was £43,000, or $215,000. Officials in Ireland had a difficult time persuading the treasury to wait until the soup kitchens were operational before they began dismissing workers.

Many British people responded enthusiastically to the new plan to set up soup kitchens in Ireland; the kitchens were already a popular way to help the poor in England. The French chef at London's exclusive Reform Club, Alexis Soyer, offered to set up a model kitchen in Dublin. Already a public figure in London because of his charity work, Soyer had created a recipe for an inexpensive soup that he distributed to a few hundred of the London poor. Soyer claimed that a daily serving of his soup, along with a biscuit, was enough to keep a person healthy and strong. Queen Victoria's own doctor disagreed, pointing out that the soup did not include many nutrients needed by the human body and that a mainly liquid diet day after day was not healthy.

Nevertheless, the Lord Lieutenant of Ireland accepted Soyer's offer of help, and his kitchen opened in April 1847, only three months after passage of the Soup Kitchen Act. The Dublin soup kitchen consisted of a canvas building with a door at each end. In the center of the room stood a 300-gallon soup boiler and a large oven. Long tables filled the rest of the room. Holes cut out of the tables held 100 quart-size enameled metal soup bowls with spoons attached by chains. First the bowls were filled with soup; then a bell rang, and one hundred of the people lined up outside were admitted. They sat on benches at the tables, and after grace was given they ate the soup. When the bell rang again, their time was up and they were handed a quarter pound of bread or biscuit as they left. The bowls and spoons were sponged off, and the whole process repeated within a matter of minutes.

On opening day, the gentry came to watch the soup kitchen in operation in return for a donation to charity. To herald the event, the British flag flew from the roof of the kitchen, drums were beaten, and the horns were sounded. A Dublin newspaper reported that "the ladies Ponsonby and many other fair and delicate creatures assembled; there were earls and countesses, and lords and generals, and colonels and commissioners and clergymen and doctors." For upper- class English and Irish, the soup kitchen was both a charity and form of novel entertainment. Within a week of the grand opening, Chef Soyer returned to London. The kitchen was turned over to the local relief committee, and as many as 8,750 people a day were served there. In order to be eligible for free soup, a person had to be penniless and have less than a quarter acre of land.

In other areas, relief committees struggled to collect enough taxes to establish soup kitchens. By late spring,

kitchens were up and running throughout the country. By midsummer of 1847, they were feeding three million people a day, and the death rate slowed.

Soup recipes varied a great deal from one kitchen to another. While some was made with nourishing meat and vegetables, other varieties contained little more than boiled water. Many kitchens served a kind of hot cereal called "stirabout" made from corn meal, rice, or oatmeal.

Some Protestant clergymen used soup as a way to win Catholic peasants away from their church. "Soupers," as these ministers were called, offered schools for children, where they would receive a free meal of soup and religious instruction along with lessons in reading, arithmetic, and other subjects.

There were, however, Church of Ireland clergy who did not agree with this movement or its methods. In

The Irish Question, 'what to do with and for the millions starving in Ireland?' was hotly debated by English politicians. Some saw it as God's will coming down upon the impure and undeserving Irish hordes; that would eliminate Britain's responsibility to its colony. A smaller population in the country would also handily support Britain's long-term plans for land reform.

rural areas, Catholic priests and Church of Ireland pastors worked together for the good of the people. However, the soupers further exasperated anger and distrust between the faiths. While Catholic priests warned their followers not to take the soup, some peasants took what the Protestants offered, although with apprehension. Others feared to accept soup from anyone at all and starved to death rather than take the chance that by eating it they would compromise their faith and suffer an eternity of damnation.

In the summer of 1847, because of financial problems, the English government decided that it could spend no more public funds on Ireland's famine. British leaders believed the worst of the famine was over anyway, since in the past no failure of the potato harvest had lasted more than two years and the potato plants that summer looked healthy as they grew in the fields.

Sir Charles Trevelyan and his colleagues had already shifted much of the financial burden of Irish relief to the landlords. These increased taxes had caused an additional burden for estate owners, who were struggling because two years of potato blight had left many tenants unable to pay their rents. In June the government passed the Poor Law Extension Act, which made landlords responsible for paying the taxes of all their tenants whose land was worth less than £4 ($20) a year.

The act forced Irish landlords to choose between paying taxes for the poorest people on their estates or evicting them. It is likely that the British government was aware that the new law would result in evictions, and is probable that the government desired such an outcome without appearing directly responsible for it. England wanted to create a new agricultural system in Ireland that was based on fewer people living on the land.

The Poor Law Extension Act changed the rules for famine relief, forcing starving Irishmen to choose between receiving help and giving up legitimate claims on land. Under the new law, anyone who was physically capable of doing work, if work was available, had to enter a workhouse in order to get food. But, if the person held more than a quarter of an acre of land, he had to give up the land before he was allowed into the workhouse. The act forced smallholders to make a very difficult choice. The land was their only hope for the future, but they were facing starvation in the present. Many gave up their land and faced despair and often death in the workhouse; others chose to die in their homes.

The act was strictly enforced. In one instance in County Offaly, the local doctor found a woman in her cabin boiling weeds for food. Her husband was in prison for debt, she had explained, and she had nothing else to give her hungry children to eat. In that area, not many people were very needy, and the doctor arranged for the children to be admitted to the workhouse, where they would be fed. At the next meeting of the workhouse's governing board, however, the doctor was charged with acting improperly. Because the children's father was tenant of nearly two acres, more than the quarter-acre the law allowed, his children were not eligible for the workhouse. It made no difference that the man was in prison and that his children were starving.

With the passage of the Poor Law Extension Act, Major Denis Mahon of Strokestown was among the landlords forced to take action. Rather than evict his tenants, he borrowed funds and offered to pay the passage for anyone who was willing to emigrate to Canada. About 810 smallholders from Strokestown accepted his offer and sailed on two ships from Liverpool, England. Unfortunately, fever broke out on both ships and many died before reaching North America. The majority of Mahon's tenants refused to emigrate or pay rent, and 3,000 were evicted. It was reported that there were 84 widows among them.

Eviction became a common occurrence all over Ireland the autumn of 1847. Often, several families in a settlement were turned out on the same day. The landlord's agent would arrive with eviction papers signed by a magistrate. He usually brought along British police or soldiers and "drivers," who were Irish peasants hired to force the people from their homes. The agent would read aloud the names of those to be evicted. People who refused to leave were forcibly dragged out, along with any furniture or possessions, and the hearth fire put out.

Sometimes the women would kneel before the agent and plead for mercy. Occasionally he would relent, but most often he gave the order for the house to be "tumbled." Several men would destroy the cabin by sawing the roof beam part way through to weaken it, fastening a long rope around the beam, and then, from outside the house, tugging on the rope until the roof collapsed into the center of the house. Sometimes the evicted woman would kneel again and pray for ill fortune to those who had left her family homeless. She might also pronounce a curse upon anyone who tried to live in that place until the day when she or her descendants inhabited it again.

The newly homeless were told to go to the workhouse and other tenants warned not to take them in, since the landlord would still be charged for them. Because the workhouse might not have had room for an entire family, many families were not willing to be separated. They would use rafters and thatch from their roofs and build lean-tos, called "scalpeens," in

secluded places. Others would create low shelters inside the walls of their ruined houses. Sometimes, their starved bodies were later discovered there.

In November of that year, while riding home in an open carriage from a meeting of the Roscommon Relief Organization, Major Mahon was shot and killed. That evening, peasants signaled the news of his murder by burning straw on the hills around Strokestown. The next night, bonfires of celebration could be seen for miles. Authorities eventually convicted two men of the crime. On the day they were hanged, hundreds of people turned out in support of them. Five other landlords were also assassinated that year.

The potato harvest of 1847 did not suffer from the

Landowners needed rent from the peasants to pay taxes. When the potatoes failed, cottagers could not raise food to sell or eat themselves to be able to work. With no money to pay rent, their homes were 'tumbled.' The roof of a house was removed to prevent a family from using the lodging and the families themselves were also removed from the farms they needed for survival.

Public works gave Irish laborers small wages to construct often useless structures. Here, two men build a stone wall. This type of relief aide often sapped the little remaining strength from peasants. Workers often fell dead on the jobsite only to be replaced by another volunteer waiting nearby.

blight. However, only a quarter of the potato fields had been planted that spring, so food was still in short supply. Two groups actively distributed food during this time—the British Association, a private charity supported by wealthy Englishmen, and the Society of Friends, or Quakers as they were commonly called. Some landlords and other wealthy individuals also ran soup kitchens. The Marquess of Sligo and his friend, Sir Robert Gore-Booth, imported a shipload of meal, shot game on their estates, and combined the two to make soup in large boilers set up on Lord Sligo's terrace.

Some resident landlords forgave rents or halved

them. One landlord forgave all rents for two years. Another 70 percent of the landlords did not live on their estates and never witnessed the suffering caused by their eviction orders. Some did observe heartlessly. A few days before Christmas of 1847, about 120 families who lived on the property of Mr. Walshe in the village of Mullaroghe, County Mayo, were evicted. The landlord's men, backed up by British soldiers of the 49th Regiment, drove 500 men, women, and children from their homes in a hail-storm, and then pulled down the buildings. Irish work-houses could not take in the large number of homeless, and hundreds of thousands died of exposure while wandering the roads in the icy winter of 1847.

THE LADY'S NEWSPAPER

LITERATURE — ACCOMPLISHMENTS — DUTIES — AMUSEMENTS — NEWS.

With which is incorporated the Pictorial Times.

No. 107.]   SATURDAY, JANUARY 13, 1849.   [PRICE 6D.

CAUSES
OF
EMIGRATION
IN
IRELAND.

WHATEVER obscurity shrouds the exciting causes of those extensive migratory movements, from time to time, among men, which history records as having so influenced the destinies of nations, the almost general abandonment of Ireland by her peasantry and lower-class farmers, in the present day, may be accounted for by a conjunction of circumstances evidently preordained. We shall, therefore, in the present article upon the condition of Ireland, exclude from prominent consideration the commonplace stock arguments founded upon presumed bad government, an impracticable national character, or a demoralizing religion. We look beyond the surface of current events and opinions, and see in the phenomenon of a whole people moved by a common spirit "to get them out of their own country," the consummation of a divine decree, whatever may have been the agency by which the extraordinary effect has been produced.

It is, indeed, the finger of Providence, pointing still, as ever, to the original destiny of man "to replenish the earth and subdue it." The old continent of Europe, occupied by conventional right, and the land partitioned to individual owners, may be truly said to be populated to excess. The lower orders of its inhabitants, in every state poverty - stricken and miserable, is proof of this, whilst to romantically, to propose a reinstitution of property to equalise fortunes more alike is an absurd condemnation of divine intention in things as they are, and any attempt to establish such a vain theory could only end in revolution and retributive ruin. A humble reliance upon the justice of Heaven and calm contemplation of the ample means from afforded man, to escape from adverse circumstances deducible from external relations over which he has no control, and not occasioned by his own misconduct, is the best

THE CAUSES OF EMIGRATION IN IRELAND.

spirit in which to meet the social evils under ably pressing upon comfort, and very exi ence, of individuals. C best illustration of this afforded by the prese state of Ireland, and t common-sense comme tary upon it made those most affected, t crowds of Irish emigra daily leaving their nat country for the uncco pied but fertile fores land, prairie, and bush The neighbouring con nent of America offers those energetic and se sible enough to take a vantage of the opportu nity offered, to repair th fortunes and to resto to them domestic happ ness and social peace.

America, in its situa tion so favourable to ceive a current of em gration issuing from I land, is, in fact, in condition, as regards cupation, the exact coun terpart of over-crowd Europe. From th mouth of the Shann to the river St. Lawren is only a seven-days' s with a fair wind; an in a properly - orders and well-sustained sy tem of emigration, in tending emigrants mig be conveyed across t Atlantic, and provisio ed during the voyag for 10s. a head. Most those proceeding to C nada even now, by i dividual exertion, an without combinatio among themselves, se dom pay more th £2. 10s. each for the passage. Who, there fore, will deny that, hardships and misfor tunes have visited th people of Ireland wit greater severity tha the inhabitants any other country the wind has not bee tempered to the nake condition of the flock, that man, persecuted an condemned, has not ther been favoured by Hea ven with a ready mean of escape from misery We see, therefore, gre reason in the circum stances of the times t believe them ordaine for facilitating the di semination of civilize Christianity throughou the fertile lands, whic over the whole glob have been prepared b divine benevolence an foresight, for the suppor of our species and th extension of human hap piness. The harsh, un couth texture, but ligh

The Lady's Newspapers carried an article on the causes of emigration in Ireland in January 1849. Culturally, one's home and hearth was a peasant's whole world; most had never left the town where they were born. It was especially difficult, therefore, to leave Ireland for an unknown land.

Leaving Ireland

Before 1846 most Irish peasants could not imagine ever leaving their native place and the neighbors and friends they cherished. They stubbornly endured discrimination and scorn from the British, although they fought back from time to time. Many of the poor died from starvation as a result of the first blight. When another wave of blight struck, the Irish began to believe their country was doomed, and some chose either to flee from it or risk dying from it. They began to sail away from Ireland in droves, weeping as they watched the Irish shoreline fade from view.

As most peasants had never been away from the town in which they were born, the journey of emigration was especially difficult. First, they had to go to a seaport and buy passage on an oceangoing ship. If they could afford it, most chose to immigrate to the United States, an English-speaking country that was free from British rule. Many others had to settle for Canada or the maritime provinces of British North America. The cost of a ticket to sleep in the hold of the ship, called steerage, ranged from £3, 10 shillings to £5, or $17.50 to $25. This passage included a small supply of water and food during the voyage.

Before the sailing date, every passenger had to appear before a doctor to be certified as healthy. The law required this inspection to prevent contagious disease from being brought on board the ship. In most examinations, the doctor merely examined a person's tongue.

Passengers were allowed to board the ship 24 hours before it sailed. If friends or relatives lived nearby, there were sad farewells. The travelers carried their belongings in bundles. Tools with which to earn a living, pots for cooking, and musical instruments, such as a fiddle, pipe, or bodhran, the Irish drum, were prized possessions. If there were musicians among them, the emigrants might have a song and dance once they got settled on board.

When the hour for sailing came, the ship was towed down river by tugboats. Meanwhile, the crew searched for stowaways. If found, they were sent back on a tug and taken before a judge. Anyone whose hiding place was not discovered would wait a few days until the ship was at sea before coming out. Since he could not be sent back, he would be assigned the most unpleasant shipboard duties to pay for his passage.

During the voyage, the ship's captain had absolute authority over every person on board, passengers as well as the crew. Disobedience could be charged as mutiny and punished by hanging. Some captains were humane, but others were bullies and tyrants who mistreated the helpless emigrants, even withholding food and water from them. Although abuses were sometimes reported, few captains were held accountable.

In the ships' holds, the wooden bunks were intended to hold four to six passengers each. Adults had about 18 inches of bunk space, and children got half as much. Passengers were advised to bring a mattress, but many slept on straw and clothing. Families would share bunks, while single men and women would be assigned randomly and could be forced to share a bunk with strangers of either sex.

When the weather was fair, passengers came on deck during the day to enjoy the fresh air, wash clothing, clean themselves, and take turns cooking at brick-lined fireboxes. At sunset a seaman put the cook fires out by pouring water down on them from his place in the ship's rigging. There were no bathrooms. Sanitation was poor,

An Irish family leaves Cork, Ireland, to emigrate to America. Before they sailed, the departing emigres would attend a party called an American Wake with their family and friends who were staying behind. Similar to a funeral wake, the participants knew they would never see each other again.

especially in bad weather when the hatches were closed and passengers remained below deck.

In the spring of 1847, ships full of Irish emigrants set sail for the United States and Canada. The first stop for those going to Quebec was an island called Grosse Isle in the St. Lawrence River. There, to gain permission to enter the country, the passengers had to pass a medical inspection. If the passenger was ill, the standard procedure was to admit him or her to the small hospital on Grosse Isle. In this way, Canadians were protected from contagious diseases being carried into the country by immigrants.

Dr. Douglas was the medical officer in charge at Grosse Isle. In 1846 his 150-bed hospital had cared for twice as many patients as usual. During the winter, Dr. Douglas had read newspaper accounts of the worsening conditions in Ireland. He feared what would happen the following spring when the ice on the St. Lawrence melted and ships began to arrive. The government did not share his concern and gave him only a small portion of the money he requested to prepare the station in advance.

On May 17, 1847, the first ship of the season reached Grosse Isle. It was the *Syria* and it carried 241 Irish passengers. There were 84 cases of fever on board. A total of 9 passengers had died on the voyage, and a 10th died on arrival. Dr. Douglas estimated that 20 more would get sick, which meant that patients from this ship alone would take up two-thirds of his hospital beds.

Ships continued to arrive daily. By May 31, there were 40 ships waiting to stop at Grosse Isle, waiting in a line stretching two miles long along the St. Lawrence River. About 1,100 cases of fever and dysentery were on the island; patients were housed in the hospital, a quarantine shed, tents, and the island's little white church. Many more sick people were on board the ships, because there was no place on Grosse Isle to put them. Even though the

ships' holds were washed down and aired, because infected lice were still present in the clothing of the immigrants, healthy passengers on the ships became infected as they waited to disembark at port.

Four doctors died on Grosse Isle that summer, and at one time or another all of the doctors were ill. Dr. Douglas asked a priest named Father McQuirk to try to recruit some nurses from among the healthy passengers. The women had such fear of the fever that none would agree to serve in spite of his appeal to their sense of Christian charity and a promise of high wages.

By the end of July, any immigrants who appeared healthy were sent on to Montreal without having to stop at Grosse Isle. As a result, typhus epidemics broke out there and in other Canadian cities. In fact, Irish immigrants who remained in good health had a hard time finding work,

Irish emigres await transport to a new land and a new life. The voyage itself was fraught with danger, though. On one ship of 241 passengers awaiting processing in Canada, there were 84 cases of fever on board, 9 had died enroute, and 20 more would soon fall ill. For the safety of people on land, sick passengers had to be quarantined and fully recovered before they could leave the processing center.

because Canadian farmers were afraid the newcomers might be carrying disease.

In September, the number of patients on Grosse Isle finally began to decrease. On October 30, the station closed. Dr. Douglas and 18 members of his staff later had a monument erected on the island in a wooded valley that had become an immigrant cemetery. The dedication reads:

> In this secluded spot lie the mortal remains
> of 5,294 persons, who, flying from pestilence
> and famine in Ireland in the year 1847,
> found in America but a grave.

Canada reached out to the survivors and quickly established soup kitchens, poor houses, and orphanages. Canadian families adopted many Irish orphans. Even so, many of the Irish were too starved and frail to survive the long Canadian winter. It is estimated that 109,000 people left Ireland for British North America in 1847. Approximately 17,000 died on the way and were buried at sea. During this period, 20,000 Irish émigrés died in Canada, including Grosse Isle.

That same year, an estimated 300,000 Irish went in search of work in England. As they crowded into the cities, there were outbreaks of typhus. In Liverpool, where the largest number of Irish went, £4,000 was raised at an emergency town meeting to send some back to Dublin.

Rather than evict their smallholders, a number of landlords paid the fare for them to emigrate. This was a good business decision, because the cost of passage was a onetime expense, much less than it would have cost to support people in a workhouse. The people selected for emigration were often the least useful workers on the estates—the very young and the aged. In December 1847, authorities in Canada protested to the British Colonial Secretary that Irish landlords were shipping off the old, sick, and penniless to Canada, where the government and private charity were obliged to help them.

Meanwhile, the government of the United States was growing increasingly frustrated by problems caused by the influx of Irish émigrés in America. One official declared that the United States was being made the poorhouse of Europe. In response to the growing numbers of Irish, the U.S. Congress passed laws reducing the number of passengers a ship could carry from the British Isles to America and increasing the price of the passage. Nevertheless, tickets to America continued to sell out.

Authorities tried to enforce the rules that protected ships' passengers, but there were too many ships and too few inspectors during the first years of famine emigration. Ships sailed that were old, unsafe, overcrowded, unsanitary, and lacking in sufficient amounts of food and water. They became known as "coffin ships," because they sometimes sank or housed so many who were dying of disease.

Stephen de Vere, a County Limerick landowner who sailed from London to Quebec in April 1847, described the scene aboard his ship:

> Hundreds of poor people, men, women and children of all ages from the driveling idiot of 90 to the babe just born, huddled together without light, without air, wallowing in filth and breathing a fetid atmosphere, sick in body, dispirited in heart . . . living without food or medicine except as administered by the hand of casual charity, dying without the voice of spiritual consolation and buried in the deep without the rites of the church.

Peasants from rural areas of Ireland who survived the ocean voyage were bewildered when they disembarked in America. The glazed look in their eyes and the style of their clothing, which was decades out of date, identified them as immigrants. The most fortunate were those with relatives or friends already established in the New World. The less fortunate found themselves taken advantage of, sometimes by fellow countrymen who were dishonest and desperate enough to cheat the new arrivals out of whatever money they had managed to bring with them.

The Ford family of Madame, County Cork, was one of many families that emmigrated to America in 1847. Three older brothers had left Ireland 15 years earlier and had established farms in Dearborn, Michigan. Leaving their cottage on an estate owned by an English landlord, the rest of the Fords walked 30 miles to Cork with their belongings and the younger children in a handcart. The group included Rebecca Ford, a 71-year-old widow; her son John, his wife Thomasina, and their seven children; and John's brother Robert, his wife, and four children.

Most likely the journey to Cork took two to three days. Thomasina Ford's parents, the Smiths, lived in a small cottage in Fair Lane, close to the docks. The emigrants stayed with them overnight before boarding a ship bound for Quebec. Perhaps there was a farewell party on that last evening. Since it was likely that those who were sailing and those who remained in Ireland would never see each other again, such an occasion was called an "American wake." (An Irish wake was a funeral vigil that is accompanied by drinking and merriment to celebrate the life of the deceased, as well to grieve the loss of the individual.)

During the sea voyage, or soon after the family arrived in Quebec, Thomasina died, most likely of typhus. The rest of the family continued on to Dearborn, and a year later John purchased an 80-acre farm from a man he had known in County Cork. John's eldest son, William, married the daughter of another family from Cork and settled on a farm of his own.

The first of William's six children, Henry, was born in 1863. Henry did not like farming, but even as a child he

was attracted by engines. In 1903, at the age of 40, he sold the first Ford motor car and went on to revolutionize American industry by introducing mass production in his automobile factories.

Sixty-five years after his family had emigrated from its famine-devastated land, Henry Ford visited Ireland. In 1912, he visited the farm where his forefathers had worked the land, and then traveled to Fair Lane, where the Smiths' cottage, since pulled down, had stood. When he returned to America, Henry brought with him the hearthstone from the fireplace of the Ford cottage and had it placed in the wall of Fair Lane, the mansion he was building in Dearborn. One of the most successful car models his company built was called the Ford Fairlane in tribute to his Irish heritage.

Henry Ford, the grandson of Irish immigrants, founded Ford Motor Company. He poses in one of his automobiles with wife Clara Bryant and grandson Henry Ford II. Ford named his large estate and one of the most popular cars, the Fairlane, after his ancestors' home in Ireland. Many influential descendants of similar immigrants became an energetic force in the United States.

A woman begging at Clonakilty in County Cork. Many peasants didn't die of starvation but of 'famine fever.' This illness was actually caused by lice and unclean conditions, though probably their malnourished bodies could little withstand infection. Peasants forced to leave their homes and sell their clothing had no way to maintain good hygiene.

Silence in the Land

One day, in 1847, Bríde Sheáin came home to her cabin with some food. As she entered, she called out to her 16-year-old daughter, but there was no response. The emaciated child lay motionless on a heap of straw, and Bríde knew as soon as she touched her cold arm that her daughter was dead.

For a while, Bríde and her husband had been able to keep their family alive by eating limpets and periwinkles that washed up from the sea. But that food was not enough. One by one the children and their father had grown silent and unseeing, then had lapsed into unconsciousness from which they never awoke.

Bríde set down her things. She poured some water into a bowl, washed her dead child as best she could, and dressed her. Then, she went to the garden. From the little haycock there, Bríde took some hay and twisted it until she had a rope that would hold together. She tied the body of her daughter on her back, using the rope to hold her in place.

As Bríde passed by the cottage of Nora Landers, Nora saw her and the burden she was carrying. Taking seven potatoes from a little pile set aside for seed, Nora pushed them under the cinders of the fire to bake. Then, she watched and waited for Bríde's return.

When she reached the church, Bríde put down her daughter. She wanted to dig a grave, but had no shovel. Two neighbors, Eamon Sheehy and Gregory Ashe, saw her and came over to help. The two men buried Bríde's daughter without a coffin, for there was none. When the grave had been filled in with dirt, Bríde spoke to her dead family. "God bless you now, all of you," she prayed. "Nobody else will join you now. There is only me left and there will be nobody to look after me to bury me here or somewhere else." Then Bríde turned and went back the way she had come.

Nora came out to meet her. "You have had a terrible time," she said, "and life is harsh and dark, but come in a while." Bríde entered and sat by the fire. Nora offered her the baked potatoes and a mug of milk. Alone of all her family, Bríde Sheáin would survive the famine and live on into old age, making a living from spinning.

■   ■   ■   ■

Death and despair were everywhere in Ireland, but like Bríde Sheáin those who survived continued to press on. In the spring of 1848, people who had managed to hold on to land planted potatoes again. Since there had been no blight the previous year, they hoped it was gone for good. But in June rain began to fall day after day and by mid-July the potato fields turned black. For many, it was the final blow. They gave up their claim on the land and asked for help.

British sympathy for Ireland was lower than ever, largely due to the radical activities of Young Ireland. This was a group of young intellectuals and political activists who had first banded together in 1842. In 1846 they had left the Repeal Movement started by Daniel O'Connell, the peace-loving, charismatic Irish leader who worked to repeal the Act of Union nearly two decades earlier, and that was now controlled by his son, John. The split occurred because the Young Irelanders would not pledge against resorting to rebellion.

Another fundamental difference between the Young Ireland and the Old Ireland, as O'Connell's supporters were known, was that the latter group was closely allied with the authority of the Roman Catholic Church. Although some of the Young Irelanders were Catholic and some were Protestant, none of the members wanted to be led by church authorities. Their original ambition was to provide new leadership and find a way to force the British to repeal the Act of Union, which, passed in 1800, had cemented Ireland under complete British control.

In 1847, an obscure Irishman named Fintan Lalor wrote to Charles Gavan Duffy, editor of Young Ireland's newspaper, *The Nation,* suggesting that the potato famine had created an entirely new situation in Ireland. It was the land that mattered now, not repeal, and "forever henceforth, the owners of our soil must be Irish." Lalor believed that the social disruption caused by the famine created an opportunity for land reform—the opportunity for the Irish to gain land back from the British. And to do so would require armed rebellion against the English. He thought the Irish were already suffering so horribly that they would be willing to combat Britain, a great world power. The Young Irelanders welcomed this new idea.

The Nation encouraged discussion and debate on Irish voting rights and home rule, as well as the redistribution of land to the Irish people. By 1848 Young Ireland was calling for complete independence from England, and Gavan Duffy was arrested. From his jail cell he wrote a call to arms that was smuggled out and printed. It read, in part, "It is a holy war to which we are called—against all that is opposed to justice, and happiness, and freedom."

Another member of the group, John Mitchel, encouraged violence against British soldiers and officials, and published a recipe for homemade bombs. Mitchel accused the British of deliberately starving the people of Ireland since they continued to export food out of the Ireland during the famine. He too was arrested. Meanwhile, the British moved tens of thousands of troops into position to prevent rebellion in Ireland.

A third Young Irelander was William Smith O'Brien, a landowner and descendent of the legendary High King, Brian Boru. Although lacking military experience, Smith O'Brien decided to single-handedly raise an army of Irish peasants. He planned to force the government to negotiate with armed rebels, but he had little success. The starving people, most of whom had never traveled more than 15 miles from their homes, had no concept of an Irish army. When he was able to gather groups of men, it was usually because they mistakenly thought he was going to feed them.

On the July 30, there was a clash between 50 British

policemen and a group of Smith O'Brien's volunteers, who were armed with guns, pikes, cudgels, and stones. The police retreated to the farmhouse of a Widow McCormack, and one rebel was killed. Smith O'Brien was soon arrested, and the rebellion of 1848 was over.

As a result of this minor uprising, the government refused any further aid to Ireland. During the first two years of the famine, England had spent £8 million on relief, and authorities believed the Irish should be grateful for what the people had already received. Instead, government leaders complained, British assistance was being repaid with rebellion and calls for independence. In September, government officials discontinued all grants to relief organizations that were out of funds and notified them that there would be no distribution of clothing to the workhouses, as had occurred the previous winter.

At the same time the Quakers also gave up in their attempts to feed people, but for an entirely different

Death wagons picked up corpses in 1847. Many authorities now agree that the famine disaster was not only caused by an agricultural fungus. English colonial policies forced the Irish people off their land and into desperate poverty, suffering, and ultimately, death.

William Smith O'Brien helped lead the 1848 Young Ireland rebellion that called for complete independence for Ireland. But his starving supporters had no experience and had not ever traveled more than a few miles from their homes. A clash between British policemen and O'Brien's volunteers quickly ended and O'Brien was arrested.

reason. The need to feed people had grown much greater than the group's ability to meet it. The Quakers did not halt their efforts to help the Irish, however. From this time on they would give the Irish assistance in the form of seed and fishing equipment, means by which the poor could support themselves.

Now, Ireland's middle-class tenant farmers, shopkeepers, and craftsmen began to emigrate in large numbers. Their country destroyed, they feared that if they stayed they too would be ruined. Entire towns stood nearly empty. Estates were neglected, their gardens and lawns overgrown and acres of farmland unplanted.

Thanks to new laws passed in 1848 and 1849,

estates could now be sold even if their owners were in debt. However, the value of land was so low that the sale price often did not even cover the cost of the mortgage and debts owed by the seller. Those who previously had been middlemen and agents for the old landlords bought up the cheaply priced properties. Then, even though they were often Irish, the new owners often raised rents and evicted people without mercy, just as the British had done.

In the spring of 1849, as reports of starvation in Ireland continued to come in, the British government decided to take action towards bringing relief. It responded by passing a new law requiring unions with enough funds to support their workhouses, and making relief services give money to other regions too poor to meet their own needs. This law requiring the Irish to redistribute funds left the country alone to resolve its dilemma of how to provide relief for its starving citizens. No more aid would come from England.

At the same time, however, British Prime Minister Russell offered a donation to the Society of Friends for whatever relief effort they were planning that year in western Ireland. The Quakers politely declined the money, explaining that its members would do nothing further, as the need had surpassed the ability of private charity to address. Only the government, maintained the Quakers, could raise the funds and carry out the measures that were necessary in many districts to save the lives of the people.

In August 1849 Queen Victoria of Great Britain paid her first visit to Ireland. Prince Albert and four of their children traveled with her. The visit was planned as a way to set Irish trade, which had come to a complete standstill, in motion. The royal family was criticized for spending money on entertainment, instead of funding nourishment for the starving people in its midst. On the whole, though, the visit was uneventful. Despite their difficulties with the English, some Irishmen, primarily those of the upper class, were willing to acknowledge the Queen as their ruler. They only wished that she would acknowledge and help them.

Cheering residents crowded the streets of Dublin and Cork, the two cities Queen Victoria visited. The gentry held receptions and balls, and well-dressed peasants danced an Irish jig in her honor. After she returned home, the Queen made a modest contribution of £200 to charity for the Irish. (She had previously subscribed £2,000 to the British Association when it first formed in response to the first appearance of the potato blight.) British policy toward Ireland remained unchanged by her visit, however, for she did not control the government; Parliament did.

The Ireland of 1849 that Queen Victoria did not see was inhabited by starving people, begging and even screaming for food in the streets of little towns. Dressed in rags, sometimes half naked, they walked the roads to the workhouses, passing dead bodies on the way. Too often, the workhouses were out of funds or even closed down. Then there was nowhere to go but back to their cabins to die in despair.

Evictions continued for many years. And, those who had nowhere to go but the workhouses continued to die of diseases they contracted there. There is no specific date when the Great Hunger ended, but, by 1852, the suffering had surpassed its peak and the number of fatalities began to decline.

In 1851, a census was taken in Ireland. Ten years before, the population had been counted at more than eight million. If the potato famine had not occurred, there should have been an increase to 9 million by the close of the decade. Instead the count was 6.5 million.

According to the census count, the population decreased in every county except Dublin. Losses were heaviest in the west, where a third of the population had disappeared. In rural Ireland, there were no barking dogs, no roosters crowing to signal the dawn, no neighbors calling out to one another. Those who remained were struck by the silence.

Annie Moore and her brothers, from Ireland, were the first of 17 million immigrants to be processed at Ellis Island, a quarantining and processing center in New York City harbor for people entering the United States. Many Americans can trace their lineage to such determined Europeans that made the difficult voyage in 'coffin ships.'

After the Great Hunger

Historians estimate that, as a result of the Irish potato famine, one million people died in the country, while another million and a half had emigrated from Ireland. Through death, eviction, and emigration, the population of the country was greatly reduced. With fewer people, more acreage was available, and farms increased in size. In 1870 and 1881, the British Parliament passed land-reform legislation, and ownership of the great estates transferred from landlords to independent farmers.

The mass emigration that had begun during the famine continued for many decades, reaching its peak in the 1870s, when nearly one-sixth of the population left the country. Most émigrés started a new life in the United States, where they hoped to escape the desperate poverty at home. Those who remained in Ireland married later in life, if at all, and had fewer children. By 1900, the population of Ireland was only four million, half its size in 1841.

The potato famine left the economy of the country in ruins, and it took many years for Ireland to recover from the disaster. During the famine years, many farmers had shifted towards grazing cattle instead of growing food crops. With fewer men competing for work on the farms, wages increased. Eventually, industries were established in Ireland, creating new jobs.

Still, economic recovery was slow, but as land reforms were instituted in the late 1800s, farmers moved from cattle-grazing and small-scale crop farms toward dairy farms. In the north, shipbuilding yards and linen mills created new job opportunities, although such positions were usually available only to non-Catholic loyalists. Over the years, gradual improvements in modern transportation resulted in the construction of ports, railroads, and airports, which also encouraged private enterprise.

The same time that the struggle for economic stability was taking place, Ireland was also striving to obtain status as a nation separate from the United Kingdom. In 1916 an attempted uprising in Dublin on Easter Monday fed the fervor that eventually led to the founding of the Irish Free State, achieved in 1922. (At the same time the province of Ulster to the north retained ties with Britain, becoming Northern Ireland.) Nationhood for the Republic of Ireland was achieved in 1948. Meanwhile in Northern Ireland bloody conflicts continued between Protestants and Catholics, with both sides responsible for acts of cruelty and violence.

The Republic of Ireland's entry into the European Economic Community (a loose economic confederation of European nations designed to make trade between countries easier) in 1972 was an important milestone. It provided an opportunity for Ireland to move away from dependence on trade with England and widen its circle of economic allies and potential partners.

As Ireland's economy grew stronger, the tide of emigration eventually reversed. Since 1996 figures show more people moving to Ireland from America than the other way around. Ireland's population has risen to five million, and the prospect for peace is encouraging descendants of Irish emigrants to return to the land of their ancestors.

The Great Hunger had a huge impact on the United States, as it was the destination of the majority of Irish emigrants. During the famine years, the city of Boston, with a population of 100,000, received 30,000 Irish within a 12-month period. During the American Civil War (1860-65) Irish soldiers on both sides of the conflict won admiration for their courage and fighting skill. After the war ended, their children and grandchildren took jobs that were difficult and dangerous—building transcontinental railroads, working in mines, and serving as policemen and firemen in the cities. Irish women found work as cooks and maids for wealthy families. Many others became nuns and taught in Catholic schools.

By 1900 the population of New York City had become one-quarter Irish. The newcomers were not always warmly received, since they were perceived as carrying disease and, because of their large and hungry families, likely to place a public burden on society. Most Irish immigrants were Roman Catholics, and during the time of mass immigration into the United States, most Americans were Protestants who believed that Catholicism, with its allegiance to the Pope, was a danger to democracy. The general prejudice against the Irish was summed up by the acronym NINA on help-wanted posters. Everyone knew that it meant, "No Irish need apply."

Familiarity with secret societies and resistance against authority in Ireland prepared the Irish to become a major force in the growth of labor unions at a time when American workers had no legal rights to a safe working environment and for job security. During the late 19th century and the turn of the 20th century Irish American labor activists gained political power in the cities of the eastern United States.

For the most part Irish Americans did not forget their loved ones back in Ireland. During the desperate years

IRISH NATIONALISM

After the great famine, many Irish people supported the idea of Ireland as an independent nation. In 1905 the political party Sinn Fein, which means "Ourselves Alone," was formed to advance the cause. It became influential in the movement toward independence and is still important today. Not all Irish favored separation from England, however. The split occurred, as it had for centuries, along religious lines—with Protestants favoring union with England and Catholics opposed.

Because of the British effort to settle loyal English subjects into the more rebellious northern part of Ireland (in the province of Ulster), the majority of residents there eventually became Protestant—English Anglican and Scottish Presbyterian. Catholics remained the majority in the other three provinces of Ireland.

When Catholics campaigned for home rule and even for complete Irish independence, Protestants in Ireland were unwilling to go along. Most feared becoming the minority group in a united Ireland that was free from British control.

Activists among the Catholic majority rebelled against England and sought to gain popular support from the rest of the Catholic population, which supported change at the time. After Irish independence activists made a failed attempt to incite revolution in Dublin on April 17, 1916, and the subsequent public execution of the rebel leaders, the movement for independence gained more active support and political momentum.

after the famine, many in Ireland had depended on money that their relatives sent to them from America. In the 1870s as much as one-third of all the money in Ireland came from the United States. Irish Americans also generously supported organizations that worked and fought for Irish independence from Britain and on behalf of Irish Catholics in Northern Ireland.

The Anglo-Irish Treaty of 1921 created the Irish Free State, officially established in January 1922. Six loyalist-dominated counties in Ulster, or Northern Ireland, voted to remain part of the United Kingdom. In 1949 the Irish Free State became the fully independent Republic of Ireland.

Hostilities continued in Northern Ireland, where Protestants ruled with the backing of the British army and treated Catholics as second-class citizens. The Irish Republican Army (IRA) continued to wage a long guerilla war against the British in Ireland. In 1972 fighting became especially fierce and bloody during what became known as "Bloody Sunday," when an elite band of British troops opened fire on peaceful demonstrators in Derry, Northern Ireland.

Throughout the 1970s and 1980s the violence between Irish Catholics, Irish Protestants, and the British military in Northern Ireland was excessive. From time to time, there were unsuccessful attempts to make peace. Random violence and brutality on both sides became an aspect of everyday life for generations of people in large Ulster cities like Derry and Belfast.

In 1995 leaders of Sinn Fein, the political wing of the IRA, and British officials met publicly for the first time in 23 years. After nearly three years of negotiations, a historic power-sharing agreement was signed in April 1998 between Northern Ireland and Britain. However by the turn of the 21st century, the terms of the agreement had still not been met.

In 1960 the great grandson of a famine immigrant from County Wexford who died of cholera in a Boston slum was elected president of the United States: John Fitzgerald Kennedy. Kennedy's election was celebrated by Irish Americans and Roman Catholics, because it marked their full acceptance into American society.

In 1997, British Prime Minister Tony Blair made a historic apology to the descendants of the Irish potato famine. He acknowledged that those who governed in England at the time of the famine had stood by while a simple crop failure turned into a massive human tragedy:

> The famine was a defining event in the history of Ireland and of Britain.
>
> It has left deep scars. That one million people should have died in what was then part of the richest and most powerful nation in the world is something that still causes pain as we reflect on it today.
>
> Those who governed in London at the time failed their people through standing by while a crop failure turned into a massive human tragedy.
>
> We must not forget such a dreadful event.

This admission may have served to ease the bitterness felt by Irish and Irish Americans.

Some of those descendants are still unwilling to close the matter. They agree with the accusation made by Young Irelander John Mitchel that England's policy was one of deliberate genocide. Indeed, thousands of shiploads of food were exported from Ireland to England while a million Irish people died of starvation. However, some modern economic historians counter this interpretation with other facts. They note that during the famine years, food was imported into Ireland as well as out of the country. And further, the aid given by the English government in 1845 and 1846 could be considered generous, coming as

it did during a time when help for the poor was not popularly viewed as a public responsibility. The fact remains, however, that when the need continued to be overwhelming, the British government abruptly ended all public relief assistance in Ireland.

Potato growers remained at the mercy of the *Phytophthora infestans* fungus for 40 years. In 1885, farmers discovered that a spray of copper sulfate and quicklime, called Bordeaux, was effective against a similar deadly fungus that had been destroying grapevines in France's vineyards. This mixture also worked against potato blight. Farmers could control the disease, although it was not eradicated.

The fungus continues to cause crop damage to this

Soldiers of the Irish Free State fight Republican forces during the Irish Civil War of 1922. Establishment of the Free State gave political independence to three Irish provinces. The fourth, northernmost province of Ulster became Northern Ireland; it remains under full British control to this day.

day. In the early 1980s, a strain of *Phytophthora infestans* emerged. Because it was resistant to the fungicide that had been developed to control the infection once it attacked the plants, many potato crops were lost in various parts of the world, including North America, Europe, the Middle East, and Far East. In the United States, the blight surfaced in Idaho, where potatoes were an important crop, and in the Pacific Northwest. Fortunately neither Ireland nor any other country in the world depends entirely on the potato as its main food source.

By the time signs of infestation appear, it is too late to save the crop. Therefore, some farmers use fungicides as a preventative measure. This is not an ideal solution because of the potential harm these chemicals can have on the environment. Research on ways to prevent blight continues. Plant scientists have developed at least one new variety of potato that is genetically designed to have a high resistance to blight.

Most people agree that the underlying cause of the Great Hunger was not really the blight on the potatoes. The deaths and suffering resulted from England's inadequate response to the loss of the potato crop. British colonial policies effectively forced the Irish people off their land and into desperate poverty and suffering.

A memorial to the people of Ireland who died during the great famine can be found at Strokestown Park, the estate once owned by Major Denis Mahon, which contains a famine museum. Among the exhibits is an explanation of the similarities between the Irish potato famine and other famines that are occurring today. The major theme is that famine results when people of poor countries are forced by ruling elite to live in poverty on undesirable land. When a natural disaster such as drought or flooding occurs, hundreds of thousands of people can die of starvation. Like the Irish peasants of the 1840s, they are victims of economic

Approximately 1.5 million Irish emigrated from the island. In their new homelands, Irish immigrants were looked down upon as generally lazy, untrustworthy, uneducated, and poor. And because of all those traits, they were thought to be a burden on their adoptive countries. Even if they proved steady and hardworking, they were accused of taking jobs and opportunities away from other laborers.

systems that put profits above the needs of humanity.

Today, a prosperous Ireland offers aid whenever famine and disease strike somewhere in the world. Ireland's president in 1997, Mary Robinson, was among the Irish government officials to make significant efforts in famine relief throughout the world. Her efforts earned her the appointment of High Commissioner for Human Rights of the United Nations.

The blighted Irish potato fields of more than 150 years ago are not forgotten. Scholars continue to explore the data to better understand the past, and humanitarians apply its example as an argument for justice on behalf of those who are desperately impoverished and restricted from the most basic human rights.

A memorial statue to Irish famine victims standing in Cambridge, outside of Boston, Massachusetts, was unveiled in 1997. This first American memorial to Irish famine victims deserves to reside near a city of 100,000 people during the famine years that absorbed an additional 30,000 immigrants in one year.

Chronology

8,000 BC	The first people arrive in Ireland
350 BC	The Gaels arrive; their language and traditions give rise to the Irish culture
432 AD	St. Patrick returns to Ireland to convert the Gaels to Christianity
795	The Vikings begin two centuries of raids in Ireland
842	First Viking-Irish alliance
1002–14	Brian Boru reigns as High King of Ireland
1170–71	Strongbow and his Norman army arrive; Strongbow becomes king of Leinster; King Henry II rules England and, claiming English rule over Ireland, allows Anglo-Norman invaders to continue fighting Irish tribal kings for cattle and land.
1367	The Statutes of Kilkenny prevent English settlers from adopting Irish language and customs
1537	Irish Parliament passes Act of Supremacy, which establishes Henry VIII and his heirs as head of a state Church of Ireland
1541	Parliament declares Henry VIII King of Ireland
1558	Queen Elizabeth I comes to power
1560	The Second Act of Supremacy is passed, by which Queen Elizabeth requires the Irish to renounce Catholicism and give allegiance to the Church of Ireland
1600	South American plant, the potato, is introduced to Ireland
1601	Nine years of war end with English victory at the Battle of Kinsale
1641	Catholic-Gaelic subjects rebel, demanding a return of lands
1649	Oliver Cromwell's army arrives in Ireland, massacring thousands of Irish and distributing their land to his followers; the Irish surrender after three years of war; thousands of Irish are banished to Connacht
1685	James II, a Catholic with whom the Irish ally themselves, ascends the English throne

Chronology

1688	William of Orange forces the removal of James II from the throne and becomes king
1690	James's army is defeated at the Battle of the Boyne; the Treaty of Limerick guarantees some rights to Catholics
1695	Catholics hold 14 percent of Irish land; penal laws prevent Catholics from receiving education or from holding office in the government or army; Roman Catholic priests are banished from Ireland
1800	Act of Union proclaims complete union of Ireland with Britain and disbands Irish Parliament
1829	The last of the penal laws is repealed
1835	The British government holds its Poor Enquiry on poverty in Ireland
1837	Victoria becomes Queen of England and Ireland
1838	The Poor Law Act establishes workhouses for Irish poor
1842	Independence-minded Irishmen form the Young Ireland movement
1845	Blight appears on potatoes throughout the country; the Great Hunger begins
1846	Potato crop fails completely; British government establishes a public works program; first deaths from starvation occur in October; a poor harvest throughout the Europe continent causes high prices on food; mass emigration from Ireland begins
1846–47	An early and fierce winter strikes Ireland and Europe; famine fever begins to spread
1847	Soup kitchens open; Britain discontinues the public works program
1847	*May:* Ships of emigrants to Canada begin to arrive at Grosse Isle, overwhelming the quarantine station with cases of fever
1847	*June:* The Poor Law Extension Act makes landlords responsible for taxes of poorest tenants, resulting in mass evictions
1847	*Fall:* The potato harvest is healthy, but small crop can't support starving population

Chronology

1848	*July:* Members of Young Ireland rebel against British oppression
1848	*Fall:* Potatoes are blighted again; emigration increases; land values drop; evictions continue
1849	Potatoes are blighted; England passes a rate-in-aid law and refuses further help
1849	*August:* Queen Victoria visits Ireland; government policy remains unchanged
1851	A census of Ireland indicates a population decrease of one and a half million from ten years earlier
1870s	Irish emigration reaches an all-time high
1905	Reform minded Irishmen form the political party Sinn Fein
1915	The Irish Republican Brotherhood and its military council, the Irish Republican Army (IRA), emerge, dedicated to forcing Britain to give up control over Ireland
1922	Irish Free State established, by which a degree of political autonomy is granted to three Irish provinces; province of Ulster becomes known as Northern Ireland and remains under full British control
1948	The Republic of Ireland emerges from the Irish Free State as a fully independent nation, while Northern Ireland remains under British rule
1997	British Prime Minister Tony Blair apologizes to the descendants of the Irish potato famine

Further Reading

Books and Periodicals

Allen, Mike. "Ireland, New Promised Land." *New York Times,*
31 May 1998.

Duffy, Seán, ed. *The Macmillan Atlas of Irish History.* New York:
Macmillan, 1997.

Durant, Will and Ariel. *The Age of Napoleon: A History of European
Civilization from 1789 to 1815.* New York: Simon and Schuster, 1975.

Fry, William E., and Stephen B. Goodwin. "Resurgence of the Irish
Potato Famine Fungus." *Bioscience,* June 1997.

Gribben, Arthur, ed. *The Great Famine and The Irish Diaspora in
America.* Amherst, Mass.: University of Massachusetts Press, 1999.

Guttman, Robert J. "What They Said . . . The Rebirth of Europe."
Europe, September 1999.

Hull, Eleanor. *A History of Ireland and Her People,* vol 2. London:
G. G. Harrap, 1926.

Lampton, Christopher F. *Epidemic.* Brookfield, Conn.: Millbook
Press, 1992.

Laxton, Edward. *The Famine Ships: The Irish Exodus To America.*
New York: Henry Holt, 1997.

Ó Gráda, Cormac. *Black '47 And Beyond: The Great Irish Famine In
History, Economy, and Memory.* Princeton, N.J.: Princeton University
Press, 1999.

Poirteir, Cathal, ed. *The Great Irish Famine.* Chester Springs, Penn.:
Dufour Editions, 1999.

Woodham-Smith, Cecil. *The Great Hunger: Ireland 1845–1849.*
Middlesex, England: Penguin Books, 1991.

Young, Arthur. *A Tour In Ireland.* London: Cambridge University
Press, 1925.

Further Reading

Websites

The Great Irish Famine
http://www.nde.state.ne/us/SS/irish_famine.html

View of the Famine
http://www.vassun.Vassar.edu/~sttaylor/FAMINE

Irish Potato Famine Page
http://www.geocities.com/willboyne/nosurrender/Potatcom.html

American Family Immigration History Center
http://www.ellisislandrecords.org

Information and Resources Related to the Irish Struggle for
National Independence
http://users.westnet.gr/c~cgian/irish.htm

Index

Index

Picture Credits

page

2: Corbis
10: © Sean Sexton Collection/ Corbis
13: © Patrick Jones/Corbis
16: Archive Photos
19: Corbis
21: Archive Photos
24: © Leonard de Selva
26: Bettmann/Corbis
30: Corbis
34: Bettmann/Corbis
37: Hulton|Archive by Getty Images
38: Bettmann/Corbis
42: Hulton-Deutsch Collection/ Corbis

45: Bettmann/Corbis
46: Hulton|Archive by Getty Images
49: Hulton|Archive by Getty Images
52: © Sean Sexton Collection/ Corbis
58: Bettmann/Corbis
63: Corbis
67: Hulton|Archive by Getty Images
68: © Sean Sexton Collection/ Corbis
70: Hulton|Archive by Getty Images
73: Corbis

75: Bettmann/Corbis
79: Associated Press, AP
80: Hulton|Archive by Getty Images
85: Hulton|Archive by Getty Images
86: © Sean Sexton Collection/ Corbis
90: ©Jan Butchofsky-Houser/ Corbis
97: Associated Press, AP
99: Corbis
100: Associated Press, AP

Cover Photos: Corbis

CAROLE S. GALLAGHER earned her B.A. in English from Wilson College, after balancing family, job, and school for several years. She believes that children need to learn about the past in order to understand the present and, someday, to shape the future. *The Irish Potato Famine* is her second book for Chelsea House. Her late husband, Donald, was a second-generation Irish-American, and their four children—James, Daniel, Kevin, and Anne—are proud of their Irish heritage.

JILL McCAFFREY has served for four years as national chairman of the Armed Forces Emergency Services of the American Red Cross. Ms. McCaffrey also serves on the board of directors for Knollwood—the Army Distaff Hall. The former Jill Ann Faulkner, a Massachusetts native, is the wife of Barry R. McCaffrey, formerly a member of President Bill Clinton's cabinet and director of the White House Office of National Drug Control Policy. The McCaffreys are the parents of three grown children: Sean, a major in the U.S. Army; Tara, an intensive care nurse and captain in the National Guard; and Amy, a seventh grade teacher. The McCaffreys also have two grandchildren, Michael and Jack.